THE BEGINNING AND THE END

The BEGINNING *and the* END

Rereading Genesis's Stories
and Revelation's Visions

Michael W. Pahl

CASCADE *Books* • Eugene, Oregon

THE BEGINNING AND THE END
Rereading Genesis's Stories and Revelation's Visions

Cascade Books
An Imprint of Wipf and Stock Publishers
199 W. 8th Ave., Suite 3
Eugene, OR 97401

www.wipfandstock.com

ISBN 13: 978-1-60899-927-9

Cataloging-in-Publication data:

Pahl, Michael W.

The beginning and the end : rereading Genesis's stories and Revelation's visions / Michael W. Pahl

xii + 106 p. ; 23 cm. Includes bibliographical references and indexes.

ISBN 13: 978-1-60899-927-9

1. Bible. O.T. Genesis I–III—Criticism, interpretation, etc. 2. Bible. N.T. Revelation XII—Criticism, interpretation, etc. 3. Bible. N.T. Revelation XIX–XXII—Criticism, interpretation, etc. 4. Bible—Study and teaching. I. Title.

BS600 P2 2011

Manufactured in the U.S.A.

To my students,
past, present, and future:
you are also my teachers

Contents

Preface

IF YOU HAVE EVER WONDERED if there might be more to Genesis than fuel for anti-evolutionism, then this book might be for you. Or if you have ever thought, "Revelation has to be more than simply a roadmap for the future of the Middle East," then perhaps you will find this book to be just what you are looking for.

Genesis and Revelation tend to provoke strong reactions. Many who read the first chapter of Genesis insist the most crucial message is that the earth was created in six, twenty-four-hour days only a few thousand years ago. Some respond by maintaining that these stories of Genesis are merely ancient myths with nothing to offer us in the twenty-first century beyond a glimpse of the strange beliefs of a people long past. Likewise, many who read Revelation claim it describes God's detailed plan for particular nations and peoples of the world—focused on Israel—in a specific period of time that is just around the corner of human history. Some respond by asserting that these strange visions of Revelation are merely the results of an unstable mind or an antiquated worldview, about as useful to us today as those early stories of Genesis.

Meanwhile, as these Scripture wars heat up, many Christians are left on the sidelines, not wanting to engage in a battle they see as unproductive or misguided; still wanting to read these important texts of Scripture, but not sure how one should approach these texts after all. It can all be very confusing, and can even turn people off from reading Genesis and Revelation.

If this in any way describes where you are, then maybe this book is for you.

One purpose for this book, then, is quite simple: I hope to demonstrate that Christians can read Genesis and Revelation in a way that is both intellectually responsible (with due historical and literary sensitiv-ity) and faith-building (with significant theological and practical implica-tions). In reading the stories of Genesis and the visions of Revelation we do not need to choose between "ancient human writings" and "divinely inspired Scripture," or between "history" and "theology," or even between "science" and "faith." Such dichotomies may indeed have an appearance of wisdom, but they lack any value in making real or full sense of ei-ther the biblical texts or the world around us. This could be put another way, rather more directly: on the one hand, acknowledging and even fully embracing the very human dimensions of Genesis and Revelation—their ancient historical and literary features—need not compel us to become agnostics or atheists or secular humanists or theological liberals or what-not; on the other hand, we do not need to be aggressive fundamentalists or fanatical zealots to take Genesis and Revelation seriously as divinely inspired Scripture.

Another purpose is equally straightforward, reflecting the "faith-building" dimension just noted. I hope to provide a reading of some stories of Genesis and some visions of Revelation that is helpful for Chris-tians in thinking about who God is, what God has done and will yet do, what it means to be human in the world, what it means to be the people of God in the world, what exactly has gone wrong with the world and how God intends to fix it, and so on. I truly do believe that beginnings and endings are crucial for us as humans in how we tell our story, how we understand our place in that story, and how we then live in the world in light of that story we tell. I truly do believe that Genesis and Revela-tion describe "the beginning and the end," and that in doing so they have much to say to human beings living between that beginning and end, in any era, including our own.

So I invite you to read Genesis and Revelation along with me, to try on my reading of these texts to see how it fits, to reread Genesis's stories and Revelation's visions as if for the first time, and to hear anew what these inspired ancient texts have to say about the beginning and the end. While I have no illusions that the reading of Scripture I present in this book is some kind of perfect or complete interpretation, I do hope it will prompt Christians of any theological persuasion to pick up and read these sacred texts in a fresh yet faithful way.

Acknowledgments

MY FAMILY DESERVES MY NEVER-ENDING gratitude for their role in my writing. It is, to be sure, mostly a passive role—putting up with my tinkering on the computer in the evenings or on the weekends—but the support of my wife, Larissa, and our children, Amelia, Michael, Matthew, and Adalynne, is very real, and always encouraging.

Thank you to Lendrum Mennonite Brethren Church—my employers, my ministry partners, and my community of faith over these past two years. Your encouragement and enthusiasm for my preaching and teaching is a much-valued impetus for me in seeking to express my ideas more widely through my writing. David Williams, Wayne Wicks, and all the good folks at Taylor Seminary and the Schalm Memorial Library likewise deserve many thanks for their hospitality during a study week that Lendrum provided, allowing me to track down references and (more importantly) to take a deep breath in the midst of the demands of pastoral ministry.

Thanks are due also to Chris Spinks and the rest of the crew at Wipf and Stock for once again taking on one of my writing projects. Your expertise and professionalism are second to none, yet this takes nothing away from your ability to make authors feel genuinely valued at a personal level.

I am grateful also to those who have read even some part of some version of the manuscript for this book along the way. My wife Larissa, my brother Steven, my colleague Chris Friesen—thank you all for your input into this project. The book is certainly the better for it.

Finally, I must thank all those who first endured the ideas of this book in their rawest form: my "Revelation" classes at Prairie Bible College and in the adult Sunday school at Mount Olive Evangelical Free Church;

my "Theology of Creation" class at The King's University College; my "Digging Deep" adult Sunday school sessions at Lendrum; and most recently my art retreat sessions on "A Theology of Creating" at King's Fold Retreat and Renewal Centre. Many of the ideas presented in this book were worked out in my study in preparation for teaching these classes and seminars, and then fleshed out in the sessions themselves. The next stage of "working out" and "fleshing out" these ideas—bringing them to bear in the daily grind of real life—is still ongoing for the teacher and (I hope!) for the other participants. Thank you, my students and friends and sisters and brothers in Christ, for engaging these ideas, asking good questions, and pushing me in new directions. For all these things, this book is dedicated to you.

Beginnings and Endings and Where to Find Them

A journey of a thousand miles begins with a single step.
– LAO-TZU (CA. 604–531 BC)

If you don't know where you are going, you will probably
end up somewhere else.
– LAURENCE J. PETER (1919–1988)

IN A JOURNEY, BEGINNINGS AND endings are crucial. The end is the desired goal, the place you are trying to get to; the beginning, of course, is where you start; and both the beginning and the end determine the path you take. Sure, journeys can take unforeseen detours, venturing into unmapped territory. And sometimes the journey itself becomes more significant than the destination. Still, every journey you will ever take is in some way defined by where you have come from and where you are going.

So it is with life. The way we understand our beginning and our end, our origins and our destiny, where we come from and where we are going—all this is crucial to our identity, our purpose, our being and living in the world. This is true for us in our relationships, in our careers, in our societies, really in all of the dimensions of who we are. Families celebrate births and grieve deaths, and mark anniversaries for all these beginnings and endings, precisely because these are so essential to our understanding of who we are and what "the meaning of life" is all about. Every year countries around the world pour millions of dollars into creating nationwide celebrations in memory of their origins and crafting detailed plans to shape their destinies—all because how we understand both the past and the future determines how we live in the present. We all need a beginning and an ending, with ourselves in the middle.

Beginning, middle, and end—those are also the most basic elements of a good story, and human beings have told stories of their perceived beginnings and anticipated endings for as far back as we can know. Indeed, this is the most common way human societies have developed their collective identity and purpose and values, and passed these on to subsequent generations: telling stories of beginnings and endings, with ourselves in the middle.

All of us tell stories in order to make sense of our perceptions and experiences. The man who tells the story to his wife about his coworker's most recent failings, the patient who tells the story to her doctor of her progressing mystery illness, the boy who tells the story to his friend of his football hero's rise from injury to championship—this kind of sense-making storytelling is happening all around us, all the time. And this happens on a collective level as well, in both formal and informal ways. In churches, synagogues, or mosques, in classes, seminars, or rallies, in theaters, bookshops, or homes—in all these venues groups of people are continually telling stories among themselves to make sense of the world they experience collectively, to establish and reinforce who they are and why they do the things they do.

But the stories that give an account of our origins or a vision of our destiny are especially powerful. A nation may tell stories of the religious faith of its founders in order to emphasize to its citizens and others that such religious faith should be a necessary part of the fabric of the nation today. A company may describe a vision of its prosperous future in order to foster a culture of excellence and success in the present. A family may repeat the account of how their grandparents immigrated to their new homeland in order to reinforce the values of adaptability and hard work that made their life possible. An athlete may visualize achieving a new personal best in her sport in order to give her the confidence she needs to actually realize that goal.

Our lives are filled with stories, and the stories of beginnings and endings with ourselves in the middle are especially vital to how we make sense of the big questions of life. Indeed, it could well be said that the one who tells the stories is the one who shapes the world.

࿇

If stories of beginnings and endings are so crucial for us in defining who we are and why we are here, where should we go to learn more about these ultimate origins and final destinations?

There is no shortage of options out there. Science may fill in some of the picture, particularly if you are interested in precise thoughts on the *when* and *how* of the earth's beginnings and of human origins. But this scientific perspective does not have much to say about *who* we are and *why* we are here in light of our past and future, or our identity and purpose and values as human beings and human societies—even collectively as a human race. The scientific enterprise is an important one, to be sure, and science is a critical dialogue partner in these kinds of meaning-and-significance questions of human existence. But science is ill-equipped to consider such questions fully, as these questions assume that there is something more going on in being human than merely what can be observed and hypothesized and experimented and reasoned, that humanness is more than proteins and chemicals and neurons and organ systems. And thus, even in our scientific age many reach beyond science to answer these kinds of questions, looking to everything from ancient religions to inner intuitions to charismatic leaders to a myriad of other options.

While Christians may legitimately turn to a variety of resources for guidance in all this—human reason, personal experience, and Christian tradition, among others—Christians have always in a special way looked to the Bible to address these kinds of questions, the big "meaning of life" sorts of questions of human existence. This is because Christians throughout history have described this collection of ancient sacred writings, these Scriptures, in line with the description of the Jewish Scriptures (the Christian Old Testament) provided in 2 Timothy 3:15–17:

> The Holy Scriptures . . . are able to make you wise for salvation
> through faith in Christ Jesus. All Scripture is God-breathed and
> is useful for teaching, rebuking, correcting and training in righ-
> teousness, so that all God's people may be thoroughly equipped
> for every good work.

According to this text the Scriptures are "God-breathed" or (to use the technical theological term) "inspired." The Greek term used in this text (*theopneustos*) was a brand new one, apparently made up just for this statement, and theologians have expended much effort in attempting to understand and describe what this word means. I would suggest that the term was intended to echo a biblical story, one which we will explore in more detail in a later chapter: the story of God shaping the human form out of the ground—everyday, ordinary earth—and then "breathing into" this sculpted soil the "breath of life" so that the human form becomes a "living being" (Genesis 2:7). In a similar way, God has "breathed into" these ancient human writings we call Scripture, so that they are "alive and active," as another New Testament author describes any true "word of God" (Hebrews 4:12). Thus, the biblical writings are very much ancient human writings; this "inspiration" does not diminish the historical, human dimension of the Bible at all, including the ways the biblical writings reflect their ancient cultures and languages and literary styles and so on. But for Christians the biblical writings are more than simply ancient human writings: God worked through their human writers—and indeed still works through their words—so that what they wrote communicated what God wants to say, both to the originally intended readers and to God's people through history, including today.

Thus it is appropriate—even absolutely vital—for Christians today to continue looking to these ancient human writings, these God-breathed texts, for "teaching, rebuking, correcting and training in righteousness," to become "wise for salvation through faith in Christ Jesus." It is fitting and even necessary for Christians to look to the Bible for guidance in answering the deeply significant *who* and *why* questions of human existence, understanding our beginning and our end, our origins and our destiny, where we come from and where we are going, in order to shape how we understand our identity, our purpose, our being and living in the world.

Two of these inspired biblical writings have been especially significant for Christians in looking back to our origins and looking forward to our destiny: Genesis and Revelation, appropriately the first and the last books in the Christian biblical canon. "Genesis" is a book of "beginnings," a book of firsts for humanity shaped by the tools of an ancient Israelite worldview. "Revelation" is a book that "discloses" or "unveils," a book of endings for humanity viewed through the lens of an early Christian perspective. Together these biblical writings sketch out a story of God, humanity, and all creation, a narrative that moves from the beginning to the end with ourselves in the middle, a narrative that calls us to live in a certain way, shaping our identity and our values in light of our origins and our destiny.

IN THE BEGINNING . . .

No river can return to its source, yet all rivers must have a beginning.

— NATIVE AMERICAN PROVERB

Imagination is the beginning of creation. You imagine what you desire, you will what you imagine, and at last you create what you will.

— GEORGE BERNARD SHAW (1856–1950)

The artist is the only one who knows that the world is a subjective creation, that there is a choice to be made, a selection of elements.

— ANAIS NIN (1903–1977)

The whole difference between construction and creation is exactly this: that a thing constructed can only be loved after it is constructed; but a thing created is loved before it exists.

— CHARLES DICKENS (1812–1870)

If you want to know the end, look at the beginning.

— AFRICAN PROVERB

Reading Ancient Origins Stories

Once upon a time ...

ONLY FOUR WORDS. YET THESE four words, placed at the beginning of a story, are evocative. They set the stage for a story of a princess and a prince, a story of mysterious magic and true love, a story ending with equally evocative words: *and they all lived happily ever after.*

If you are a native English speaker raised in a Western society, chances are you will immediately know the genre: it is a particular kind of folk tale commonly called a fairy tale, made popular by a wave of animated Disney films over the past century. Not only that, but you will know exactly what to do with this story, how to interpret it. You would not take the opening "once upon a time" literally, as if the narrated events really did happen at a particular time and place in human history. Nor would you put much stock in the final "and they all lived happily ever after"; if you thought about the words at all, you might smile ruefully to yourself, since "happily ever after" is so rare in real life. Rather, you would read the story as a fictional tale intended to entertain or, at most, to reinforce certain social values—the importance of making good moral choices, maybe, or perhaps a societal ideal of romantic love.

But we can look a little deeper. How does truth work in such a story? The fairy tale is not "true" in the sense that it accurately relates events that happened in human history. But the fairy tale does have its own kind of truth: like all texts, its truth is related to its purpose. As we have just noted, a fairy tale is supposed to entertain, or perhaps to support certain social ideals. If the fairy tale does indeed provide the promised entertainment, then in a very pragmatic sense it can be said to be "true." More significantly, if the values it reinforces are in fact good and useful within the particular society in which the tale is told, then in a more profound sense it can also be said to be "true."

We can push these reflections even further. How do you know these things? How do you know that this story is a fairy tale—that it did not actually happen, that it should not be taken literally, that it is intended for entertainment or social reinforcement? Again, if you are a native English speaker raised in a Western society chances are you know all this intuitively. Sure, you may have formally studied fairy tales at some point, but quite likely you picked up on most of this already as a child, even if you could not have expressed these ideas at that time in quite this way. If, however, you are not a native English speaker raised in a Western society, you would have to learn about fairy tales in order to make good sense of them.

All this is related to what is perhaps the most crucial key for interpreting any text, whether ancient or modern, secular or sacred. That interpretive key is understanding the text's *genre*, or the kind of literature it is.

A genre is like an implied contract, an unwritten agreement, between the author and the reader of a text. The genre establishes a framework, certain conventional guidelines or constraints, for creating and understanding the text. The author of a text works within the conventions of that particular genre, perhaps stretching those guidelines in some new directions, but still in a way that is recognizably that genre. She will indicate the genre through a variety of means—none explicit (the author will not start off announcing, "This is a fairy tale"), but rather implicit: through characteristic words or phrases or topics or themes, or through such features as the piece's style or length or structure. Once you recognize the genre—whether intuitively or through careful determination—you are better equipped to interpret the text, to discern whatever truth (or even goodness or beauty) it may convey.

So you will interpret a history textbook differently than a historical novel, even if they speak of the same historical setting. You will read a newspaper editorial differently than a front-page report, even if they are on the same topic. A Shakespearean sonnet will make a very different impression on you than a vehicle's mechanical manual, even if you really love that car. And you will understand and experience the truth of a cookbook in a very different way than you would the truth of a chemistry textbook, even if they describe the same chemical processes.

But if you miss the text's genre, you will miss the text's purpose, and that can get you into all sorts of trouble. Woe to those who mistake historical fiction for a history textbook! (Remember *The DaVinci Code*?)

                                                 ∽

Genesis is certainly not a modern folk tale or fairy tale, but what *is* the genre of Genesis? If you were a librarian 2,200 years ago in the ancient library of Alexandria in Egypt, where would you put your newly acquired scrolls of Genesis? Should it be placed alongside the Greek histories of Thucydides, or with the fables of Aesop, or perhaps beside the narrative geographical sketches of Patrocles?

If you were that ancient librarian, more than likely you would place Genesis alongside writings known today as *Enuma Elish* and *Atra-Hasis* and *Gilgamesh*, primeval stories from ancient Mesopotamia. Mesopotamia is the region between the Tigris and the Euphrates rivers, essentially where modern-day Iraq is, and extending up into Syria. Babylonia was the most prominent of the ancient Mesopotamian kingdoms at least as it relates to ancient Israel. Ancient Egypt itself had similar primeval stories inscribed on stone walls and coffins (making it a little hard to fit them into Alexandria's library!), but these stories were later copied and collected together with other religious writings in what is known as the *Pyramid Texts* and the *Coffin Texts*. All these primeval stories could be called "etiological narratives"; that is, they depict in story form "why things are the way they are," describing the nature and function and purpose of common realities in the storyteller's lived experience (realities such as deities, religious worship, human beings, ethnic groups, languages, and so on) by telling a story of the origins of those realities. A more specific type of these etiologies is a "cosmogony," an account of the origins of the earth and life on earth from the perspective of the storyteller or her community.

Ancient etiologies and cosmogonies such as *Enuma Elish* and the stories in the *Pyramid Texts* were not so much concerned with the precise *when* and *how* of these origins, or whether the stories happened in history exactly as described—though undoubtedly many ancient Babylonians and Egyptians believed the world had been made just as their stories said. Rather, these stories functioned at a deeper level to shape the worldview of these peoples by answering the *who* and the *what* and the *why* of human existence in the world: Who are the gods? What is the world? Who are human beings? Why do human beings exist? What is our purpose related to the gods and the world and one another? What (if anything) is wrong with the world? How (if at all) can things be made right? This is in fact the way truth works in such ancient etiologies. *Enuma Elish*, for example, reinforced some important values for ancient Babylonian culture: that the gods are personalized manifestations of nature, strong but capricious; that the natural world is therefore powerful but indifferent toward the fate of human beings; that human beings were created to serve the mightiest god, Marduk, by appropriate temple ritual; that human beings can function as servants of Marduk to stem the tide of chaos in the natural world; and so on.

Genesis, then, is an ancient Israelite etiology, and the creation stories of Genesis 1–2 are more particularly ancient Israelite cosmogonies. In fact, these Genesis creation stories resemble the ancient Mesopotamian and Egyptian stories of origins in many respects. This should be expected considering that these two cultures—one directly to the northeast and the other directly to the southwest of Israel—were extremely influential in every other way on ancient Israelite society. As the geographical bridge between these two regions, Israel could not help but breathe the same cultural air as Babylon and Egypt. So, for example, the ancient Mesopotamian and Egyptian language of "image" used for filial, royal representation is reflected in Genesis 1, and the Babylonian picture of human beings created out of clay mixed with the divine essence is paralleled in Genesis 2. Also, for example, these ancient origins stories think of creation in terms of cosmic order being brought out of primeval chaos, a notion shared by the first creation story of Genesis. More specifically, these ancient cosmogonies are very concerned to demonstrate that this created order has a strongly religious element, and even that a crucial focus of this order is a temple built to the god or gods in which ordered religious practices must be performed to bring about order within broader society and the world. This idea is also shared by the Genesis creation stories, with all creation ordered and filled to be God's temple—as we will explore in the next chapter.

But the Genesis creation stories do not simply parrot the older stories of Mesopotamia and Egypt. Rather, while they share certain motifs and language with these other stories, the stories of Genesis boldly present themselves as the alternative to all other origins stories, describing the one true God, his work in the world, and his purpose for humanity and the created order. Thus, for example, these Genesis stories are unapologetically monotheistic, describing only one true God as opposed to the many gods and goddesses of Egypt and Mesopotamia. And so also these Genesis stories emphasize God's distinctiveness related to nature: unlike the Babylonian and Egyptian concept of the gods as personalized forces of nature (such as the sky and sea and land), Genesis 1 emphasizes that God created these natural features, that these forces of nature are not God but are rather created things under God's sovereign control.

We will explore more of this in the coming chapters, but for now this brief introduction to the striking similarities and profound differences between Genesis and other ancient etiologies underscores the kinds of questions Genesis was intended to answer—or, one could say, the way truth works in these Genesis stories. As an ancient etiology (including ancient cosmogonies), Genesis was not written to respond to questions of precisely *when* or *how* everything came to exist. Like those in surrounding cultures, undoubtedly there were many ancient Israelites who believed everything came into existence just as their creation stories described—but this is not the *point* of these stories. The first creation story of Genesis 1, for example, uses the pattern of seven "days" as an organizing principle for describing the ordering of God's cosmic temple (reflecting the weekly rhythms of ancient Israelite life, with six days of work and one day of worship-rest), but we should take just as seriously the second Genesis creation story using the language of a single "day" to encompass all God's creative work ("In the day that the LORD God made earth and heaven," 2:4). Each statement is intended to make a deeply theological point, a point related to the questions Genesis *was* intended to answer, questions of *who* and *what* and *why*.

One important indication that we are on the right track in seeing these as the key questions these stories are intended to answer is that later biblical texts glance back at these foundational origins stories to answer precisely these questions, and not others. The Christian Scriptures are filled with references to these stories—quotations, allusions, echoes— and none of these later Scriptures employ the first stories of Genesis to describe exactly *when* or *how* creation came about. "The heavens declare the glory of God," the psalmist affirms (Psalm 19:1). Israel should know "from the beginning" that God "sits enthroned above the circle of the earth" (Isaiah 40:22); indeed, God declares, "Heaven is my throne, and the earth is my footstool. Where is the house you will build for me? Where will my resting place be? Has not my hand made all these things, and so they came into being?" (Isaiah 66:1–2). "Since the creation of the world," Paul says, "God's invisible qualities—his eternal power and divine nature—have been clearly seen" (Romans 1:20). These and other biblical appeals to the natural world or the creation stories are made to emphasize *who* God is, *who* and *what* human beings and the rest of creation are, and *why* God has made all things and continues to care for all things.

Thus, we risk doing a grave injustice to the inspired, sacred text of Genesis when we try to make it answer *our* questions of precisely *when* and *how*. God created all things, to be sure—God himself and not merely some impersonal forces or natural laws—this is affirmed not only in Genesis but throughout the Christian Scriptures. But Genesis was simply not intended to answer the sorts of modern questions Christians have of exactly when or how God created all things. We are not taking the text of Genesis *more* seriously by trying to make it answer these questions; we are in fact taking the text of Genesis *less* seriously, forcing it to answer our questions, rather than making its questions our questions and submitting to the answers it was intended to give. If we truly wish to hear the voice of God through the text of Genesis, if we truly want these stories of Genesis to shape our thinking and our living in line with God's purposes, then we need to seek *the text's* answers to the deeper worldview questions of *who* and *what* and *why*: Who is God? What is the world? Who are human beings? Why do human beings exist? What is our purpose related to God and the world and one another? What is wrong with the world? How can things be made right?

And so it is to these sorts of questions we now turn, reading the primeval stories of Genesis to shape our theology and our practice as the people of God created in the image of God out of the stuff of earth to do God's will in his very good—though death-cursed—world.

A Story of Creation (Genesis 1)

In the beginning God created the heavens and the earth. Now the earth was formless and empty, darkness was over the surface of the deep, and the Spirit of God was hovering over the waters.

And God said, "Let there be light," and there was light. God saw that the light was good, and he separated the light from the darkness. God called the light "day," and the darkness he called "night." And there was evening, and there was morning—the first day.

And God said, "Let there be a vault between the waters to separate water from water." So God made the vault and separated the water under the vault from the water above it. And it was so. God called the vault "sky." And there was evening, and there was morning—the second day.

And God said, "Let the water under the sky be gathered to one place, and let dry ground appear." And it was so. God called the dry ground "land," and the gathered waters he called "seas." And God saw that it was good.

Then God said, "Let the land produce vegetation: seed-bearing plants and trees on the land that bear fruit with seed in it, according to their various kinds." And it was so. The land produced vegetation: plants bearing seed according to their kinds and trees bearing fruit with seed in it according to their kinds. And God saw that it was good. And there was evening, and there was morning—the third day.

And God said, "Let there be lights in the vault of the sky to separate the day from the night, and let them serve as signs to mark seasons and days and years, and let them be lights in the vault of the sky to give light on the earth." And it was so. God made two great lights—the greater light to govern the day and the lesser light to govern the night. He also made the stars. God set them in the vault of the sky to give light on the earth, to govern the day and the night, and to separate light from darkness. And God saw that it was good. And there was evening, and there was morning—the fourth day.

And God said, "Let the water teem with living creatures, and let birds fly above the earth across the vault of the sky." So God created the great creatures of the sea and every living and moving thing with which the water teems, according to their kinds, and every winged bird according to its kind. And God saw that it was good. God blessed them and said, "Be fruitful and increase in number and fill the water in the seas, and let the birds increase on the earth." And there was evening, and there was morning—the fifth day.

And God said, "Let the land produce living creatures according to their kinds: livestock, creatures that move along the ground, and wild animals, each according to its kind." And it was so. God made the wild animals according to their kinds, the livestock according to their kinds, and all the creatures that move along the ground according to their kinds. And God saw that it was good.

Then God said, "Let us make humans in our image, in our likeness, so that they may rule over the fish in the sea and the birds in the sky, over the livestock and all the wild animals, and over all the creatures that move along the ground." So God created humans in his own image, in the image of God he created them; male and female he created them. God blessed them and said to them, "Be fruitful and increase in number; fill the earth and subdue it. Rule over the fish in the sea and the birds in the sky and over every living creature that moves on the ground."

Then God said, "I give you every seed-bearing plant on the face of the whole earth and every tree that has fruit with seed in it. They will be yours for food. And to all the beasts of the earth and all the birds in the sky and all the creatures that move on the ground—everything that has the breath of life in it—I give every green plant for food." And it was so.

God saw all that he had made, and it was very good. And there was evening, and there was morning—the sixth day.

Thus the heavens and the earth were completed in all their vast array.

By the seventh day God had finished the work he had been doing; so on the seventh day he rested from all his work. Then God blessed the seventh day and made it holy, because on it he rested from all the work of creating that he had done.

[handwritten margin notes:] Two Stories — 1st & 2nd chapters

IT OFTEN COMES AS A surprise to Christians to discover that there are in fact two distinct creation stories in Genesis: the first story just narrated runs from Genesis 1:1 to 2:3, and the second is found in Genesis 2:4–25 (though the story really continues at least into Genesis 3). That these are two different stories is evident from their many distinctive features. For example, in the first story God is consistently called *Elohim* in Hebrew, meaning simply "God," while in the second he is called *YHWH Elohim*, or the "LORD God"; in the first story animals and humans are merely commanded into existence by God (1:20, 24, 26), while in the second story they are shaped by God from the earth (2:7, 19); and in the first all this happens over six "days" (1:3–31), while in the second all this is summarized in a single "day" (2:4, literally, "In the day that the LORD God made earth and heavens").

We cannot be certain when these stories were first told, but many scholars suggest the second story is actually the older of the two. In any case, it is possible that some version of both stories were told in the homes and villages of the early Israelites or their forebears well before they were brought together in the book of Genesis as we know it. These stories are distinct, but clearly at some point the ancient Israelites believed them to be compatible, or both stories would not have been included side by side in the first chapters of Genesis.

In the previous chapter we saw that ancient cosmogonies such as these were intended to answer the deep worldview questions humans have, the *who* and *what* and *why* of human existence in the world. So what does the first biblical creation story have to say to these sorts of questions?

[handwritten: 1.] First, *who is God?* "God" in this story is *Elohim*. This is the plural form of the generic Hebrew word for a deity or, occasionally, a human ruler. *El* is a "mighty one." The use of the plural does not mean that this refers to many gods, nor is this some kind of pre-Christian intimation of the Trinity (God as a plurality of persons). Rather, the plural conveys either an abstract concept—that God as *Elohim* is the epitome of "deity"—or it indicates an intensive or superlative idea—that God as *Elohim* is the "very strong one" or "mightiest one."

God is already there "in the beginning" (1:1). God stands before time and space as we know it; God creates within the time and space we experience. Unlike other ancient creation stories, in which the natural world comes into existence incidentally out of the conflicts of the gods or erotically out of the couplings of the gods, in this biblical creation story "heaven and earth"—everything in the cosmos—is created simply by God's divine will. God merely speaks and the pieces of creation come into being and fall into place. Furthermore, God names the most foundational created elements—the "day" and the "night" (1:5), the "sky" (1:8), the "land" and the "seas" (1:10)—indicating his sovereign control or ownership over these features of nature. This is especially significant because in other ancient cosmogonies these features are presented as gods or goddesses. In one version of the Egyptian stories, for example, the god Ra is the sun, Shu and Tefnut are air and water, Geb and Nut are earth and sky. In contrast, this first biblical creation story emphasizes that there is only one true God, and that all these features and forces of nature are not gods at all but merely creations of the one Creator God, under God's power and control.

All this underscores God's transcendence and omnipotence, or—to put this in "more Hebrew" terms—God's holiness and his might. God is "holy"—completely other than all else that exists—and no one should confuse God with the natural world he has created. God is "transcendent"—beyond the constraints of this time and space, which he has created. And God is "almighty" or "omnipotent"—able to do anything he wills to do. In short, God is *Elohim*, the "mightiest one," who creates and rules over all things by his sovereign will and power.

So then, *what is the world?* To answer this question we need to explore the way the story is structured.

The story is introduced with the well-known statement, "In the beginning God created the heavens and the earth." This is either a summary statement for the whole story ("God created all things, and let me describe that to you in more detail") or it is a statement that God created the cosmos and that it was first in the chaotic state described in the next verse: "formless and empty." In any case, this pair of words is crucial for the story, echoing ideas of other ancient creation stories in which order is brought about from a primeval chaos. This means that what follows in the story is all about God conquering chaos and bringing order to the cosmos, forming and filling his initially "formless and empty" creation (1:1–2).

And this is indeed what we see in the story: God moves from forming creation to filling it, focusing in repeated, parallel fashion on the elemental spheres of Light and Darkness, Water and Sky, and Land and Sea (1:3–31):

Day	Forming/Filling	General Focus	Specific Focus
One	Forming	Light and Darkness	Creation of light, separation of light and darkness
Two	Forming	Water and Sky	Separation of waters by a firmament
Three	Forming/Filling	Land (and Sea)	Creation of land, separation of land and sea; creation of vegetation from the land
Four	Forming/Filling	Light and Darkness	Creation of heavenly lights, separation of light and darkness
Five	Filling	Water and Sky	Creation of water and sky creatures
Six	Filling	Land	Creation of land creatures; creation of human beings

This structure and progression emphasizes the order and abundance—the perfect "fittingness"—of creation. These ideas are also highlighted by the six-fold pattern of the particular days themselves, the story again underscoring by its very structure the concepts of order and abundance:

- "And God said, 'Let [X happen],' and it was so": creation by command, indicating obedience to God as sovereign Creator, usually along with some further description as well.

- "God called [X Y] . . . ": naming the created elements, indicating ownership and control over them.

- "God saw that it was good": a divine aesthetic assessment, or an assessment about the "fittingness" of creation.

- "And there was evening, and there was morning—the Xth day": reflecting back on the human work day from dawn to dusk.

Thus, in this first creation story God conquers the primeval chaos and crafts a highly ordered and abundant creation, forming it and filling it so that it is a suitable . . . *something*. What exactly is it that God builds?

A temple. In creating the heavens and the earth God builds a perfect sacred space for himself, the holy and almighty *Elohim*. In other ancient cosmogonies various aspects of religious worship are prominent. In the *Enuma Elish*, for example, the culmination of the order brought out of chaos is the proper worship in Babylon of Marduk, the god who brought about that order in the world. A variation of this creation story was used for the dedication of sacred buildings in ancient Babylonia. In stark contrast to these other ancient stories, however, in Genesis 1 there is no particular geographical location or humanly constructed building that functions as God's temple. All creation is God's sacred space; the entire cosmos is God's dwelling place. Nothing else could be "very good" or perfectly fitting for the holy and almighty Creator God.

All this helps to make sense of why it is that this creation account is structured around six days (1:3–31), with a seventh day of rest set apart as sacred (2:1–3). Within the story, these are actual days, not "epochs" or long periods of time. They are undoubtedly intended to parallel the weekly pattern of the ancient Israelites: six days of work primarily in the natural world of fields and vineyards, followed by a seventh day of rest or "Sabbath" as a sacred act of worship, including temple worship. But the point of this weekly pattern was to emphasize the Sabbath: the six days of work move forward to the seventh day of rest, culminating in this holy day set apart for rest and worship. In a similar fashion the creation account of Genesis 1 emphasizes that all God's acts of creation move forward to the sacred seventh day in which God the Creator is worshiped in his holy temple, the cosmos which God himself has created. Thus, the ancient Israelite life of work in the world and rest in worship reflects the cosmic order of creation; these rhythms of life for ancient Israel were patterned after God's own creative rhythms of earthly work and holy rest in the sacred temple of his created order (e.g., Exodus 20:8–11).

So then, *who are human beings? Why do human beings exist? What is our purpose related to God and the world and one another?* The answer that this first biblical creation story gives to these questions is found in the culmination of the story of earth's forming and filling: the creation of human beings "in the image of God" (Genesis 1:26–27).

There are some close parallels to this language of "image" or "likeness" in ancient Mesopotamian and Egyptian texts. In this ancient context, to say that someone (a vassal king, perhaps) or something (say a statue of the king) was in the king's "image" was to say that this person or thing represented the king—reflecting his presence in that place, ensuring his will, protecting his interests. They were the king's "royal representatives" within a particular territory under their control. Even more significantly, this idea was extended back to the king himself: he was in the "image" of the gods, a very child of the gods even, representing them in the world as their priest-king. (Think of the famous child-pharaoh known popularly as "King Tut": "Tutankhamun" means "living image of Amun," a prominent Egyptian god.)

This context suggests that to say human beings are created in God's "image" or "likeness" is to say that they are God's "priest-kings" representing God as King, that they are children resembling God as Father. And indeed, this is what we find: the ideas of royal representation and paternal resemblance are clearly reflected in the Genesis language of "image" or "likeness." So in Genesis 1 the statement that human beings—both male and female equally—are created "in God's image" is immediately followed up with the statement that they are to "rule" over the creatures of the earth, to "fill the earth and subdue it"—to extend God's sovereign rule throughout the earth (1:26–28). And later in Genesis 5 we have a family genealogy in which Adam produces a son, Seth, "in his own likeness, in his own image," a family "image" or "likeness" that has just been noted as reaching back through Adam to God himself (5:1–3).

Thus, human beings—*all* human beings, not just kings and pharaohs—have been created "in God's image": created to be God's royal representatives within the sacred space of God's creation, extending God's transcendent rule throughout the earthly temple; and created to be God's children, resembling God—and relating to God—as human children do their parents, reflecting God's character, his glory, to the world. All human beings bear this "image of God," and thus each human person bears both the dignity and the responsibility of being God's "image-bearer" in the world: living in relationship with God as children with their father, living out God's character in relationship with one another and all creation, bringing God's sovereign, loving rule to bear on all things throughout the earth.

This first biblical creation story tells us nothing about exactly when God created all things or how he did so, beyond his transcendent will as ultimate cause of creation. But, as we have seen, it tells us much about who God is, what creation is, who human beings are, and what our divine purpose in the world is. What is the significance of these ideas for Christian thought and life today? Though many implications of these thoughts could be noted, let me provide three areas for further consideration.

First, *this first creation story should deeply influence the way we view God.* God is the one holy and transcendent God, completely distinct from all else that exists; God is the almighty and omnipotent God, all-powerful, able to do anything he wills to do. These truths call us away from any form of idolatry: not just bowing down to idols of wood or stone, but—much more deeply—thinking or acting in any way that displaces God from his rightful place. God is the ultimate source of our life and all that we have. God alone provides purpose to our existence, and all of humanity's deepest desires are only fulfilled in God. God is the only one outside of our most dire situations, the only one powerful enough to meet our most difficult challenges, and thus the only one who can deliver us from our most desperate predicaments. No humanly crafted ideology or entity or resource can fill these roles—neither capitalism nor communism, neither democracy nor dictatorship, neither nation-state nor natural strength, neither wealth nor wisdom—only God the Creator.

To bring this close to home, we should ask ourselves some hard questions. What do we look to as the source of our life and the good things we enjoy? Where do we turn when we lack those good things? What is it that defines our purpose for being, for us as individuals or for our faith communities? What is it that gives meaning to our life, to our work, to our rest and recreation? When we face our most difficult problems and most dire situations, where do we go for help? Is it some human resource such as money, or knowledge, or physical strength? Is it some human system or institution like capitalism or democracy, or any government? Or is it a human being, perhaps a close friend or parent or spouse? Certainly the holy and almighty God can work *through* things and people to meet us in each of these ways, but as Christians our first and final answer to these questions should be God our Creator.

Second, *this first creation story should profoundly shape the way we think about the natural world.* Nature is not merely "nature," a rather neutral term; it is in fact "creation." It is not a phenomenon brought about by random, impersonal forces and therefore without any ultimate significance. It is not a resource to be used up or exploited to fulfill humanity's never-ending desires. It is not a hostile force that must be aggressively tamed in order to build a comfortable dwelling place for humanity. It is not a temporary shelter for humanity to be discarded for something better down the road. All of these perspectives on the natural world can be found in Christian thinking, but all badly miss the reality of "nature" as God's creation, which he has affirmed as "very good." The created order is God's sacred temple, beautifully and fittingly made by God to be the place where God meets with humanity, where God dwells with his human family. It is therefore a reflection of God's glory, God's eternal power and divine nature (see Psalm 19:1–4; Isaiah 66:1–2; Romans 1:20), and so to be treasured by humanity, God's royal representatives on the earth.

This thought does, then, speak to the modern question of evolution and Christian faith, though perhaps not as directly or extensively as some might like. If we are going to allow Scripture to shape our understanding of God as Creator and the natural world as God's creation, we cannot have a purely naturalistic approach to the origins of the universe, the earth, and life on earth. That God—the holy and almighty and loving and faithful God—"created the heavens and the earth" means that we must not think of all things coming about through merely arbitrary forces or purely natural processes. Creation proceeds from God—from the will of God, from the heart of God—and thus is radiant with divine significance. While some may wish to say more than this about God's role in the process and timing of creation, as Christians we certainly cannot say less.

All this points to another, very practical application of this perspective on the natural world as God's creation: the importance of what has been called "creation care." Many Christians are skeptical of environmentalism, some seeing in this a flawed theology that attributes too much significance to nature or even "divinizes" nature. But this criticism is entirely unfounded: no biblical text so clearly differentiates between the transcendent God and the created world as Genesis 1 does, yet no text so clearly emphasizes the "very good"-ness of creation and human responsibility within God's creation as Genesis 1 does. Caring for creation in "environmentally friendly" or ecologically sensitive ways is not somehow

Interesting Point

sub-Christian; it is in fact a profoundly Christian thing to do, taking seriously the very purpose for which God created humanity in his image. Christians should be at the forefront of such efforts, not because we share in some flawed theology but because our own Christian theology—our own inspired Scripture—calls us to this task of creation care.

Finally, *this first creation story should significantly affect the way we view human beings both individually and collectively.* Each and every human being is created in God's image, and thus has an inherent value conferred by God. Each and every human being—male or female, young or old, black or white or any other shade, Christian or Muslim or Jewish or Hindu or Buddhist, disabled or able-bodied, mentally challenged or average or gifted, gay or straight, born or unborn—each and every human being is a person to be loved and respected for their own sake, not as an object to be used and manipulated for the gain of others. And each and every human being, as created in God's image, has a share in the responsibility of being in that image, living in such a way that God's character is revealed through them in relationship with God and others and that God's sovereign rule is extended through them in their corner of the world and around the globe. Collectively, humanity is a single family created by a common Father for a united purpose within a shared world. We share humanity's promise together, we face humanity's perils together, and we walk together into humanity's future.

For some Christians this might seem to be too all-encompassing, too generous, too "liberal." To this objection let me offer two comments in reply. First, it is important to remember that there are other stories yet to be told in the Scriptures—stories of human sinfulness and divine redemption—that provide additional shade and color to this opening story of creation. Second, however, we must allow the full weight of this first creation story to bear upon our understandings of humanity and the world. We must take seriously the notion that every human being bears the image of God, that all human beings are in a broad sense "children of God"—as later biblical authors in fact do (e.g., Acts 17:24–29 and James 3:9). If we do not take this idea seriously, we must ask some very pointed questions of ourselves about how seriously we are in fact taking the inspired opening creation story of our authoritative Scriptures.

But this is not the only divinely inspired creation story to be heard. We must also listen carefully to this first story's complement, to add some

In the Beginning . . .

of that additional shade and coloring to those big meaning questions of life, the *who* and *what* and *why* of God, humanity, and all creation.

A Second Story of Creation (Genesis 2)

This is the account of the heavens and the earth when they were created, when the LORD God made the earth and the heavens.

Now no shrub had yet appeared on the earth and no plant had yet sprung up, for the LORD God had not sent rain on the earth and there was no one to work the ground, but streams came up from the earth and watered the whole surface of the ground. Then the LORD God formed the human[1] from the dust of the ground and breathed into his nostrils the breath of life, and the human became a living being.

Now the LORD God had planted a garden in the east, in Eden; and there he put the human he had formed. The LORD God made all kinds of trees grow out of the ground—trees that were pleasing to the eye and good for food. In the middle of the garden were the tree of life and the tree of the knowledge of good and evil.

A river watering the garden flowed from Eden; from there it was separated into four headwaters. The name of the first is the Pishon; it winds through the entire land of Havilah. The name of the second river is the Gihon; it winds through the entire land of Cush. The name of the third river is the Tigris; it runs along the east side of Ashur. And the fourth river is the Euphrates.

The LORD God took the human and put him in the Garden of Eden to work it and take care of it. And the LORD God commanded the human, "You are free to eat from any tree in the garden; but you must not eat from the tree of the knowledge of good and evil, for when you eat of it you will certainly die."

1. In this passage I have substituted the TNIV's translation "man" with "human." In keeping with this, in one place "woman" has been changed to "female human," and in two places "man" has been changed to "male human." See page 30 below for my reasons for these changes.

The LORD God said, "It is not good for the human to be alone. I will make a helper suitable for him."

Now the LORD God had formed out of the ground all the wild animals and all the birds in the sky. He brought them to the human to see what he would name them; and whatever the human called each living creature, that was its name. So the human gave names to all the livestock, the birds in the sky and all the wild animals.

But for the human no suitable helper was found. So the LORD God caused the human to fall into a deep sleep; and while he was sleeping, he took one of the human's ribs and then closed up the place with flesh. Then the LORD God made a female human from the rib he had taken out of the human, and he brought her to the male human.

The male human said, "This is now bone of my bones and flesh of my flesh; she shall be called 'woman,' for she was taken out of the human."

For this reason a man will leave his father and mother and be united to his wife, and they will become one flesh.

The man and his wife were both naked, and they felt no shame.

ᑈ

1

THE FIRST CREATION STORY IN Genesis is all about transcendence and holiness, power and omnipotence, order and structure. The second creation story (told above from Genesis 2, but really continuing at least through Genesis 3) is a tale of intimacy and immanence, love and faithfulness, honor and loyalty—even despite a tragic betrayal and a debilitating curse. If the first creation story is a bit like a description of a grand cathedral, the second is a bit like a love story. 2.

However, while it may have some of the texture of a love story, this creation story is still an ancient cosmogony intended to answer deep human worldview questions, the *who* and *what* and *why* of human existence in the world. So what does this second biblical creation story have to say to these sorts of questions?

Who is God? God in this story is "the LORD God," *YHWH Elohim* in Hebrew. As we saw in the first creation story, *Elohim* conveys the idea of "mightiest one," emphasizing God's strength and power, God's "Godness." However, by adding the name *YHWH* (or *Yahweh*), the name of God in this story takes on a further nuance. The name *YHWH* is God's covenant name, the name God gives to Moses in a later biblical story

(Exodus 3:13–15) as the name by which God is to be known in his covenant with Israel, that mutual agreement of relationship with ancient Israel established through Moses at Mount Sinai (Exodus 19–24). *YHWH* is derived from the Hebrew for "I am," and could be paraphrased in that covenant context as "I always have been, always am, and always will be everything you [Israel] need me to be." And indeed *YHWH* proved this to be true: *YHWH* was everything Israel needed God to be, liberating Israel from slavery in Egypt, delivering them from Egypt's armies in crossing the Red Sea, establishing them as God's people keeping his covenant through Moses, and bringing them into the land God had promised to their ancestor Abraham (see Exodus and Joshua). *YHWH* is thus an intensely relational name, a name evoking potent thoughts of love and faithfulness, and a deeply salvific name, a name bringing to mind deep-seated hopes of liberation and justice.

For this second creation story the perspective shifts from "the heavens and the earth" to "the earth and the heavens" (2:4). God is right in the midst of his creation. There is no divine command from the great beyond in this story. Rather, here we see God getting his hands dirty, personally shaping his creatures out of earth and flesh with the artistic care of a sculptor (2:7, 19, 21–22), even breathing God's own life into the human he sculpts—an evocative, intimate image (2:7). And, as the story continues into Genesis 3, we see God coming to the humans he has created, seeking them out for an evening stroll in the beautiful garden designed for them (3:8–9).

All this underscores God's immanence, or—to put this in "more Hebrew" terms—God's love and faithfulness. God is "immanent"—present with, intimately near, creation—an immanence expressed in deeply personal and profoundly covenantal terms through what later stories will call God's "loyal love" (*hesed*) and "faithful righteousness" (*tsediqah*). So it is that this second creation story sets up those later Old Testament stories: the God of Abraham, Isaac, and Jacob is *YHWH Elohim*, the immanent and omnipotent Creator who shaped humankind out of clay (see Genesis 12–50); the God who redeems Israel from slavery in Egypt and brings them into a promised land is *YHWH Elohim*, the loving and loyal Creator who provides a garden paradise for humans to enjoy with him (see Exodus and Joshua); the God who will re-gather God's people from the four corners of the earth under the banner of the Messiah is *YHWH Elohim*, the faithful and righteous Creator who infuses the whole earthly creation with his goodness and beauty (e.g., Isaiah 40–55).

It is striking that this story, which so clearly emphasizes God's immanence, is set immediately on the heels of the first creation story, which so clearly emphasizes God's transcendence. While each of these creation stories may have circulated independently before being brought together in Genesis, the fact that they *were* brought together in this way suggests that the ancient Israelites understood something profoundly true and necessary about God: both transcendence and immanence are essential for how humans should think about God. Other ancient ideas of the gods as personalized forces of nature were rejected as presenting a divinity of extreme immanence. But the ancient Israelites did not simply move to the other end of the spectrum with a divinity of extreme transcendence; rather, they saw both transcendence and immanence, both distinctive holiness and loyal love, as vital to a proper understanding of God and his relationship to humanity and all creation.

We have already suggested an answer to our next question: *What is the world?* Creation as God originally designed it is a beautiful and life-sustaining garden of "delight" (*eden*, 2:8), a paradise filled with trees "pleasing to the eye and good for food" (2:9). The natural world is thus the setting in which human beings are to find meaningful existence with God, to care for creation, to enjoy creation—to exist in "peace" or *shalom*, that blessed existence on earth in harmonious relationship with God and all creation (2:8, 15; 3:8). This portrait of creation complements the first creation story in some important ways. For example, one could possibly misunderstand the Genesis 1 description of creation as a cosmic temple carefully ordered and arranged by God, taking this to imply that the natural world has merely a functional existence as an almost sterile monument to God's glorious transcendence. This would be a poor reading of Genesis 1 itself! But in any case Genesis 2 dismisses such a notion: the grand cathedral of creation is also a living garden of unsurpassed beauty and abundance.

So then, *who are human beings? Why do human beings exist? What is our purpose related to God and the world and one another?* This second creation story develops answers to these questions in different ways than the story of Genesis 1.

As we noted above, in this second story God shapes the first "human" (*adam*) from the "ground" (*adamah*). Like a potter with clay or a sculptor with stone, God the immanent Creator takes previously exist- ing material—"dust of the ground," very ordinary, very mundane—and makes a human form. Then, in an act of acute intimacy, God breathes his own breath into the form he has shaped, and the human form becomes a "living being" or "soul" (*nephesh*, 2:7). This echoes some other images from the ancient world, such as the Babylonian notion of humans created out of earth and divine blood. Both the Israelite and Babylonian stories are emphasizing through this that humans are mysteriously, paradoxi- cally both of the earth—vitally connected to the natural world—and of the divine—animated by an expression of the divine essence. To be "hu- man," then, means being in the world; being "human" cannot be divorced from being in God's created time and space on earth. But to be "human" also means having a connection to God not shared by the rest of creation, expressing something of God's nature in a way the rest of creation cannot.

These narrative accents supplement the first creation story with its idea of human beings created "in God's image." That idea could well be seen to highlight the way in which human beings reflect God's transcen- dence: God is King over the entire cosmos, and humans in his image are God's royal representatives, God's priest-kings and -queens over our cor- ner of the cosmos, the earth. This second creation story reinforces this with the idea of the divine "breath" within humans, but also adds a neces- sary dimension: humans are created "from the dust of the ground," indi- cating that, while humans may rule over the earthly creation on behalf of God, we are also a very much a part of the natural world in which we mediate God's rule. Humans thus reflect not only God's transcendence over creation, but also God's immanence within creation.

This first human, the archetypal human, is placed in the garden God has created and is given both privilege and responsibility. Humanity has the privilege of enjoying the beauty of creation and the sustenance of cre- ation's abundance: the trees of the garden are "pleasing to the eye and good for food" (2:9). But humanity is also to "work the garden and care for it" (2:15): humans have the responsibility of sustaining the created world which gives us sustenance, of nurturing the natural world which gives us such enjoyment. This unique blend of privilege and responsibility related to creation brings meaning to human existence.

This dimension of the story also supplements the first creation story. One could perhaps take the language of Genesis 1 to inappropriate ex- tremes, hearing in the language of humans "ruling over" or "subduing" creation a notion of domination or subjugation, an idea that the flow of obligation goes entirely from nature to humanity. As we have already suggested, the first story itself is at odds with this idea: human "rule" of creation is to reflect God's rule over creation, and God rules in ways that bring about good for his creation. But if one still came out of the first story with any idea of human domination or subjugation of nature, this second story completely dispels it. Extending God's rule throughout creation means (at least in part) caring for creation in very direct ways, "getting our hands dirty" in creation just as the immanent God has done.

This first human is *adam*, a Hebrew word that can mean a "male human" but often means generically "humanity" or "human." This generic sense is certainly what the word means in these opening descriptions of this second story (hence my use of "human" in modifying the TNIV text above). This becomes clear as we follow the narrative through in this chapter, but it is also underscored in a later summary description: "When God created *adam*, he made them in the likeness of God. He created them male and female and blessed them. And when they were created, he called them *adam*" (Genesis 5:1–2).

In the narrative this first human is initially "alone": there is no one of the same kind, no "suitable helper" or "corresponding force"—or perhaps more literally "facing power" (*ezer kenegdo*)—that stands as the human's equal; there is no other creature that reflects both connection with the world and connection with the divine. This is highlighted in the story by the description of the human sorting through all of God's creatures, searching in vain for an equal to share the human enjoyment of creation's beauty and abundance or the human task of working in and caring for the created world (2:18–20).

To provide just such an equal for the human, God does something we should be prepared for by now in the story: God gets his hands dirty yet again, this time shaping another human from the first human's flesh and bone (2:21–22). In this way God divides the *adam* into male and female, and each provides for the other the "suitable helper" or personal equal that is needed to work in and care for and enjoy creation. This leads to the joyful shout of the male human that the female human is "bone of my bones and flesh of my flesh" (2:23). Every time a man and a woman come together in sexual intimacy this cry of celebration is echoed; every time a husband and wife come together in lifelong commitment this joyful discovery of an equal companion is repeated—which makes sex and marriage profoundly sacred acts (2:24).

Much more could be highlighted in this story, but there is one aspect of the narrative that is crucial to acknowledge in anticipation of the story we will explore in the next chapter. This is the note of human account-ability to God, portrayed in the image of a particular tree in the garden whose fruit the first human is not to eat: "You are free to eat from any tree in the garden," the LORD God says, "but you must not eat from the tree of the knowledge of good and evil, for when you eat of it you will certainly die" (2:16–17). The idea of humans being accountable to God is already woven into these first two creation stories. Being God's royal representa-tives, God's children, those in the "image of God," carries a responsibility in relationship that implies accountability (1:26–27), as does the charge by God to "work the garden and care for it" (2:15). But in this command not to eat of the "tree of the knowledge of good and evil," a more direct note of human accountability to God is sounded in the story, one that will take on a more ominous tone as the story continues into Genesis 3.

⌐〉

As with the first biblical creation story, this second creation story tells us nothing about exactly when God created all things, or how God did so beyond his immanent presence in shaping the earth's creatures. But, as we have seen, it tells us much about who God is, what creation is, who human beings are, and what our divine purpose in the world is. What is the significance of these ideas for Christian thought and life today? Once again, many implications of these thoughts could be noted, but let me provide three areas for further consideration.

First, *this second creation story should deeply influence the way we view God*. This story, especially in concert with the first creation story, underscores the need to think about God in terms of both transcendence and immanence. The history of Christian thought reflects the problems that can develop when one takes either divine transcendence or divine immanence to an extreme without regard for the other dimension of God's relationship to creation. One extreme view of divine transcendence is deism, the idea that God created all things but then left creation to work according to its own intrinsic design without any need for his ongoing sustenance or care. Another is a form of dualism that says there is a sharp distinction, an impassable divide, between the material and the immaterial, the physical and the spiritual, the natural and the divine; and that (in the most problematic versions of this) the material, the physical, the natural must be put aside and the immaterial, the spiritual, the divine is all that will ultimately endure. Divine immanence has also been taken to an extreme, most prominently in pantheism, the idea that "all is god and god is all"—the sun, the earth, the trees, the birds: all are the divine and the divine is all. Some versions of pan*en*theism (the idea, not that "all is god and god is all," but that "all is *in* god" or perhaps even "god is *in* all") also reflect this extreme immanence, particularly those that see the divine as so tied to the natural world or its processes as to be virtually indistinguishable from them.

These sorts of understandings of God that move either toward extreme transcendence or extreme immanence create all kinds of problems for other important ideas. For example, in views of extreme divine immanence God is so bound up with humankind and the rest of creation that God cannot provide any help for us should things go awry—as in fact the next story in Genesis describes. Put simply, we need someone outside of the problems of humankind and the earthly creation to rescue us from our predicament, and an extremely immanent God cannot provide any such rescue. But views of extreme divine transcendence are no better: while God would certainly be distinct from creation and its problems, such an extremely transcendent God would not—or perhaps even *could* not—come near to rescue his creation. It may be inexplicable, even paradoxical and rather mysterious, but we need the balance of both transcendence and immanence in understanding God and God's relationship to humankind and all creation—a balance provided for us in the opening stories of Scripture.

This second creation story should also significantly affect the way we understand the nature of humanity and human sexuality. Human beings have, to a degree, been created to reflect both the transcendence and immanence of God. Of course, this should not be understood to reflect some sort of human omnipotence (being all-powerful) or omnipresence (being everywhere-present). As we saw in the previous chapter, the holy God is utterly distinct from his creation, and God alone possesses what could be called "absolute transcendence" and "absolute immanence." Rather, human transcendence and immanence is a relative transcendence and immanence, conditioned by our finiteness and conditional upon God's existence and purpose. Still, there is a real sense in which human beings—as those created "in God's image" and animated by the divine "breath"—reflect God's transcendence over creation, extending God's sovereign rule throughout the earth. And there is a genuine way in which human beings—as those "formed from the dust of the ground"—reflect God's immanence within creation, such that just as God has bound himself to creation in loving and faithful care, so also should humans be bound up with the rest of creation in God-like love and faithfulness.

This second creation story also has great significance for matters of human sexuality, even establishing later biblical perspectives on sexuality and marriage (for instance, Mark 10:4–9 and 1 Corinthians 6:15–17). Human beings are sexual beings. Sexuality is not somehow irrelevant to what it means to be human; rather, sexuality is an essential part of our humanity—we are "male and female." Moreover, we are "male and female" both equally "in God's image," both equally sharing in the "dust of the ground" and the "breath" of God. And when "male and female" come together in a lifelong commitment of intimacy and companionship, something good and beautiful is created. These divinely designed, inbuilt ideals of human sexuality, of gender distinction yet gender equality, and of lifelong marital commitment are frequently disregarded or distorted in our day and age. But this story stresses the inherent goodness of human sexuality and gender and marriage, and the fundamental equality of male and female in God's design. These are important ideals to underscore in our day and age, although the fact that this story describes these ideals in ways that were culturally specific to ancient Israel suggests that we must also be willing to allow for differences in cultural expression of these ideals.

These thoughts relate in a deep way to the above discussions of divine and human transcendence and immanence. These two creation stories of Genesis deny the legitimacy of any sort of dualistic separation between the material and the immaterial, the physical and the spiritual, the natural and the divine. This is reflected not only in the balance of divine transcendence and immanence in these stories, but also in their balance of human transcendence and immanence. To be truly divine means God is both transcendent and immanent in relation to creation; to be truly human means humans are both transcendent and immanent in relation to the rest of the natural world. And this human immanence means that to be truly human is *not* to despise our bodies, *not* to deny our sexuality, but rather to fully embrace and even celebrate these dimensions of our humanity that God has created.

Finally, to extend these thoughts even further, *this second creation story should profoundly shape the way we think about humanity's place within the natural world.* Humans are vitally connected to the earth, and vitally connected to other creatures of the earth: we, like all animals, are "of the ground"; each of us is *adam* of the *adamah*. The earth is not the set of a fleeting drama in which humans play a bit part before striking the set and leaving the play for real life beyond the stage. The earth is where real human life happens, now and in the future. Nor is there some absolute distinction between humanity and the natural world, such that we can treat the natural world as our whims lead us without any consequence to ourselves. We are of the earth, and the earth is in us, in our flesh, in our bones. This is no Eastern pantheism or tribal animism; this is the witness of Christianity's sacred Scriptures.

The importance of this connection between humanity and the earth cannot be overestimated. Everyone longs for significance; every human being attempts to derive some kind of meaning or purpose out of their perceptions and experiences of the world. This creation story affirms that any purpose or significance we may discern in being human is vitally connected to our existence in the world. The natural world—this earth— is the indispensable setting given by God for us to be human; we cannot be human apart from the body that God has given us and the world in which God has placed us. The three classic dimensions of humanity's search for meaning are *beauty, truth,* and *goodness*; everything humans consider meaningful is either beautiful or true or good, or some combination of these three. Our thoughts here suggest that these three dimensions of meaning are bound up together, and all three are inseparable from our bodily existence in the earthly world God has created as "very good." As humans of the earth, as *adam* of the *adamah*, we experience beauty, truth, and goodness not by some escape from the world, but only by fully experiencing the world as God's good creation.

But we never fully experience this meaningful human existence in the world, do we? At most we only seem to snatch glimpses of this paradise here and there as we live our lives in this earth. This is where the tragic betrayal and debilitating curse come into the narrative—and where we see even more clearly the loyal devotion that gives this tale the texture of a love story.

A Story of Sin's Curse (Genesis 3)

Now the serpent was more crafty than any of the wild animals the LORD God had made. He said to the woman, "Did God really say, 'You must not eat from any tree in the garden'?"

The woman said to the serpent, "We may eat fruit from the trees in the garden, but God did say, 'You must not eat fruit from the tree that is in the middle of the garden, and you must not touch it, or you will die.'"

"You will not certainly die," the serpent said to the woman. "For God knows that when you eat of it your eyes will be opened, and you will be like God, knowing good and evil."

When the woman saw that the fruit of the tree was good for food and pleasing to the eye, and also desirable for gaining wisdom, she took some and ate it. She also gave some to her husband, who was with her, and he ate it. Then the eyes of both of them were opened, and they realized they were naked; so they sewed fig leaves together and made coverings for themselves.

Then the man and his wife heard the sound of the LORD God as he was walking in the garden in the cool of the day, and they hid from the LORD God among the trees of the garden. But the LORD God called to the man, "Where are you?"

He answered, "I heard you in the garden, and I was afraid because I was naked; so I hid."

And he said, "Who told you that you were naked? Have you eaten from the tree that I commanded you not to eat from?"

The man said, "The woman you put here with me—she gave me some fruit from the tree, and I ate it."

Then the LORD God said to the woman, "What is this you have done?"

The woman said, "The serpent deceived me, and I ate."

So the LORD God said to the serpent, "Because you have done this, cursed are you above all livestock and all wild animals! You will crawl on your belly and you will eat dust all the days of your life. And I will put enmity between you and the woman, and between your offspring and hers; he will crush your head, and you will strike his heel."

To the woman he said, "I will make your pains in childbearing very severe; with pain you will give birth to children. Your desire will be for your husband, and he will rule over you."

To the man he said, "Because you listened to your wife and ate from the tree about which I commanded you, 'You must not eat of it,' cursed is the ground because of you; through painful toil you will eat of it all the days of your life. It will produce thorns and thistles for you, and you will eat the plants of the field. By the sweat of your brow you will eat your food until you return to the ground, since from it you were taken; for dust you are and to dust you will return."

Adam named his wife Eve, because she would become the mother of all the living. the LORD God made garments of skin for the man and his wife and clothed them. And the LORD God said, "The human has now become like one of us, knowing good and evil. He must not be allowed to reach out his hand and take also from the tree of life and eat, and live forever." So the LORD God banished him from the Garden of Eden to work the ground from which he had been taken. After he drove them out, he placed on the east side of the Garden of Eden cherubim and a flaming sword flashing back and forth to guard the way to the tree of life.

⌒

As we have seen, the two creation stories of Genesis 1–2 deal with some of the deep meaning and significance questions of human existence, the *who* and *what* and *why* sorts of questions. God is the transcendent and immanent, holy and almighty, loving and faithful Creator. The cosmos is God's good creation, the temple-like sacred space for God's presence, the garden-like overflow of God's abundance and life, the ideal and necessary setting for human beings and God's interaction with them. And humans are God's children reflecting God's character, God's ambassadors extending God's loving and faithful rule throughout the earth, God's gardeners working the earth and caring for it in all its lush beauty.

But this is not the whole story of humanity, for we all know that human existence in the world is rarely, if ever, like this paradise. At our worst times, in our bleakest moments, we may even see the human experience as a downward spiral of futility, guilt, shame, hostility, oppression, exclusion, pain, suffering, and finally death. What is wrong with the world? And how can things be made right? In this third story of Genesis narrated above—really a continuation of the second creation story from Genesis 2 into Genesis 3—we begin to see some answers to these equally important questions of human existence in the world.

You may recall the strong note of human accountability to God presented in both the creation stories of Genesis, especially underscored by the evocative image of the "tree of the knowledge of good and evil" and God's command that the human not eat of this tree's fruit, for, as God says to the human, "when you eat of it you will certainly die" (2:17). In this extension of the second story, this tree becomes the focal point for determining human destiny, through a strange yet suggestive image: a serpent successfully tempts the humans to eat of the fruit from this tree, and thus they disobey God and incur a curse. What should we make of this story?

As with both of the creation stories in Genesis 1–2, this story is told in a way that would have had maximum impact for the ancient Israelites. The serpent would have brought to mind Egypt and the evils Israel had experienced there, as the serpent was a prominent symbol of the Egyptian pharaohs, worn as a crown to symbolize their power and their protection by the gods. Just as the name "Babylon" provoked memories among later Jews of their exile in that land, and so "Babylon" became a symbol of any empire that opposed God's purposes (e.g., 1 Peter 5:13 and Revelation 17–18), in a similar way the image of the serpent would have provoked memories among these earlier Israelites of their bondage in Egypt, and so the serpent became a symbol of evil embodied in the world (see Revelation 12:9). This means that the enigmatic promise of Genesis 3:15 would in all likelihood have been read by ancient Israelites as reflecting this Egyptian enslavement of Israel ("the serpent will strike the heel of the woman's offspring") yet also Israel's redemption from Egyptian slavery through the death of the firstborn ("the woman's offspring will crush the serpent's head")—even as it points to the broader reality of evil in the world affecting the human race yet ultimately being destroyed by the offspring of Eve.

The "knowledge of good and evil" is not inherently a bad thing; it is not simply "experience of sin" or some similar notion. Nor is the serpent's statement to the woman untrue, that "God knows that when you eat of it your eyes will be opened, and you will be like God, knowing good and evil" (3:5). These things are clear from the way the story ends, when the LORD God says, "The man has now become like one of us, knowing good and evil" (3:22). Rather, the idea seems to be that this "knowledge of good and evil" is something only the Creator should have, a knowledge only the Creator can handle. "The knowledge of good and evil" is a merism, a common Hebrew figure of speech that points to a whole spectrum of realities by giving the end points of that spectrum—just as the opening phrase in Genesis 1, "the heavens and the earth," means "the skies, the earth, and all things in between." In this light, the "knowledge of good and evil" could well be understood as the awareness of the possibilities of the whole spectrum of good and evil, or, one could say, "full moral awareness." For these archetypal humans, their disregard for God's design, their disobedience of God's will—their "sin," to use the later biblical language—moves them from a moral innocence to an awareness of all the possibilities of both good and evil. This is knowledge that only God should possess. For humans this full moral awareness has proven costly, leading humanity to depths of depravity that offset any heights of beauty and truth and goodness also ascended by humankind.

The cost of this disregard for the divine will is spelled out in ways that would have made sense to ancient Israelites in an agriculture-based society built around close-knit family groups, with all the values such societies and groups hold dear. Shame in relationships—both among humans and between humans and God—is expressed in the image of nakedness (3:7, 10). Guilt in trespassing a divine command is portrayed in eating the fruit of a tree (3:11). Hostility within creation is described in terms of the relationship of a woman and a snake (3:15). Physical pain and suffering is presented in the image of a woman's labor in childbirth and a man's toil in the fields (3:16–17). Systemic human oppression is painted in the colors of a husband's domination of his wife (3:16). A sense of futility in life and work—even creation itself cursed—is conveyed in the image of thorns and thistles in the land (3:17–19). Physical death is the return of the body to the ground from which it was made (3:19). And exclusion from life as God intended it—a summary of all that has been described—is represented in terms of banishment from the ideal garden

God has made (3:22–24). All these effects of sin are portrayed in the story in ways that had maximum impact for the ancient Israelites, yet all of these things—shame, guilt, futility, hostility, exclusion, oppression, pain, suffering, and death—are the common experience of humanity in deviating from the divine design, disregarding the divine will.

These diverse effects of human sin are also described in the story with some rather ominous words: "curse" and "death." These are multifaceted ideas. The threefold "curse"—the very opposite of divine "blessing"—accounts for most of these results of human sin (3:14–19). But the language of "death" encompasses all of them. You may recall the LORD God's statement in the previous part of the story: "When you eat of this fruit, you will certainly die" (2:17). This solemn warning of "death" is fulfilled in the narrative in all the ways we have just highlighted: shame and guilt in relationships, futility in life and work, hostility in relationships, leading to oppression and exclusion, physical and psychological suffering and pain, and the cessation of bodily life. This "death," the cost of human sin, is thus not simply physical death but rather a comprehensive reality—a "deep death"—affecting individual human beings, collective human societies, and even the rest of creation (see also Proverbs 10:16; John 5:24; Romans 3:23; 5:12–21; 6:23; James 1:15; 1 John 3:14). These archetypal humans were offered the choice of life or death—the fullness of life through the "tree of life" or a comprehensive death through the "tree of the knowledge of good and evil" (2:9, 16–17)—and they chose deep death over real life.

But even in the midst of all this there is hope. God the Creator does not destroy his creation now tainted by sin, now cursed by death. Rather, God cares for the humans he has created even in their cursed state: he clothes them in garments of animal skin (3:21), covering their shameful nakedness. God will not give up on his creation; God will do what must be done to deal with the dark stain of human sin.

↩

All of these first stories of Genesis were very much written for the ancient Israelites, with this third story describing for them what is wrong with the world and hinting at how things can be made right. But what is the significance of these ideas for Christian thought and life today? Let me suggest three areas in which this story speaks to our experience.

First, *this story should shape our understanding of the reality of "sin."* Something is wrong with the world, and we all know it. Different cultures, different religions, different people may name this wrongness differently, but we are all aware of it on some level. We sense it when we witness grave injustice, when we experience personal betrayal, when we see open arrogance or blatant greed on display. The Christian name for all this is "sin": when human beings disregard God's will for humanity, distorting God's design for humanity in the world to be image-bearers reflecting God's love and faithfulness to other people, to all creation, and to God himself.

We badly miss the real significance of sin when we think of "sins" merely as an arbitrary list of random actions we must not do. Certainly specific actions can lead to negative consequences; human experience in every age is filled with examples—an act of greed damaging a future, an act of lust devastating a relationship, an act of hatred destroying a life. But these are not merely discrete acts that have no relationship to any other action; they reflect patterns of behavior deeply embedded in individuals, in families, in societies, and in the human race. This is "sin"—these deeply embedded patterns of behavior that bring damage and distortion and destruction, that degrade our humanity in God's image and deform God's design for us as human beings. Specific "sins"—the particular acts of greed and lust and hatred and pride and injustice and unfaithfulness and so on—are manifestations of the wider problem of "sin" that has affected humanity.

The tragic story of Genesis 3 is thus not merely a story of a primeval man and woman; it is both the story of the whole human race and the story of each individual person. Both the history of humankind and the experience of each individual person reflect this story of sin's curse: despite knowing that certain actions or patterns of behavior degrade our humanity or destroy our relationships or damage our world, despite knowing that alternative actions or behavior patterns can lead us to a life of healthy relationships and meaningful existence in the world, still we give in to the temptation to put our own desires ahead of the needs of others, still we give in to those devastating actions or distorting behavior patterns, and so we experience shame, guilt, futility, hostility, exclusion, oppression, pain, suffering, and death. And it happens over and over, again and again, each human story confirming the tragic story of all humanity. To borrow the Apostle Paul's words, we are all "in Adam," each of us individually and all of us collectively repeatedly living out Adam's tragic story of sin leading to death (Romans 5:12–21; 1 Corinthians 15:20–28).

But the reality of sin in the human experience does not mean that either the human race or individual humans are the worst they can possibly be. Human sin has brought the "knowledge of good and evil"—awareness of the possibilities of the whole spectrum of good and evil. Thus, the reality of sin means that the very best of humanity—both collectively and for each of us individually—is perpetually shadowed by the very worst of humanity. And perhaps most maddening of all is that humans are fully aware of this Jekyll and Hyde within us—we *know* this in our own experience. And in the end our experience of our sin-stained humanness seems always to be missing . . . *something* . . . something fully colored, fully flavored, fully *alive*.

This story should also influence the way we think about "death." Death is the great equalizer; it is the one oppression all human beings must face. And all human societies, all human individuals, seek in some way to deal with death: trying to prepare for it, to delay it, to deny it, to mask it, to avoid it.

This Genesis story encourages us to understand "death" more broadly, yet to view death more hopefully—paradoxically giving death great power yet at the same time denying death any real power. On the one hand, we should understand physical death within the broader framework of all that is wrong with the world, within that broader framework of sin and its effects noted above. Physical death for human beings is the end result of a long process of deep death, a lifelong experience of pain and suffering—physical, emotional, and psychological. However, on the other hand, we see hints in this story both of death's naturalness in this world and of a hope for God's care even through this accursed death, thus suggesting we can view death with a measure of peace and hope. The idea of humans "returning to the ground since they came from the ground" reflects a natural cycle of death that all living creatures experience. "From dust we came and to dust we will return" can give us a measure of peace, of serenity, in the face of death, knowing we are part of a cycle of life and death experienced by all living creatures. As the Teacher of Ecclesiastes notes, "There is a time for everything . . . a time to be born and a time to die . . . all come from dust, and to dust all will return" (Ecclesiastes 3:1–2, 20). But this story of Genesis also points to God's ongoing care for human beings even in their accursed state, the immanent care of a transcendent

God who transcends life and death. God is the God of the living, "for to him all are alive" (Luke 20:38)—and this can give us hope.

This story thus presents some tension with regard to physical death. On the one hand, it is portrayed as a normal part of life for all living creatures—all are "of the ground" and all "return to the ground." On the other hand, it is portrayed as an intrusion into God's created order—it is part of the "curse" of sin, part of the comprehensive "death" that results from human disobedience of the divine will. Both of these—however paradoxical it may seem—need to be part of our thinking about death. Biological death in the natural world is necessary for biological life to continue. Yet the death of each human person is a profound wrong—even the ultimate injustice—for one created in God's image.

But if biological death is necessary to biological life, and humans appeared late on the scene of earth's history, then how can death be simply a consequence of human sin when it was around, and even already necessary, before humans even existed? For the many Christians who accept scientific evidence for an old earth, this can be a troubling question. It is always important to remind ourselves that these stories of Genesis were not intended to answer these sorts of questions that arise from modern science. But it is also important to follow through on the implications that the "death" that results from sin in Genesis 2–3 is not merely physical death but includes all the consequences of human sin. This kind of "death"—a deep death that runs from shame to guilt to futility to hostility to exclusion to oppression to pain to suffering and finally to bodily death—did not exist prior to human sin. Indeed, it *could not* have existed prior to human sin, because only humans created in God's image could sin in this way, and only humans created in God's image could experience this whole range of sin's effects. The biological death of all living creatures is not what Genesis 3 is concerned with; rather, it is concerned with human death, and more specifically a wide-ranging "deep death" that impacts human relationships with God and others and all creation, with the physical death of human beings as the capstone curse of this death-filled life.

In light of all these things, finally, *this story should underscore for us humanity's and all creation's need for—and real hope for—redemption.* Many Christians have looked to Genesis 3:15 as the "first gospel" in the Scriptures, the *protoevangelium*: "I will put enmity between you [the serpent] and the woman, between your offspring and hers; he will crush your head, and you will strike his heel." This has been interpreted as referring to Jesus as the "offspring" of Eve who would "crush Satan's head" (destroy the source and embodiment of all evil) even though Satan would "strike Jesus' heel" (Jesus would be crucified). As discussed earlier, the ancient Israelites who first heard this story would not have heard anything like this, but rather more likely a reference to their own history of redemption from slavery in Egypt. However, as we also noted, it is certainly possible that this imagery does reflect something broader than merely Egypt and Israel's liberation, as the "serpent" became symbolic of all evil embodied in the world, and as "Eve's offspring" does seem to have represented the people of ancient Israel—from whom the Messiah would come, the king from the dynasty of David who would establish the kingdom of God on earth (see 1 Chronicles 17:10–14 and Romans 9:5). Thus, while Genesis 3:15 would certainly not have denoted "salvation through Jesus" for its original hearers, there is some legitimacy of seeing it as alluding to "deliverance from evil through Israel, even Israel's Messiah."

The other passage in Genesis 3 that is often "Christianized" is 3:21: "The LORD God made garments of skin for Adam and his wife and clothed them." Some Christians have made much of the fact that providing animal skins would have necessitated killing these animals—perhaps God was foreshadowing the death of Jesus to deal with the sin of humanity? Again, the ancient Israelites who first told this story would not have heard anything so specific or future-oriented in this detail. However, they may well have heard echoes of their own sacrificial practices outlined later in the books of Moses, practices that involved animals being killed to "atone" for the sins of Israel (see Leviticus 16–17). And there is little doubt that the earliest Christians interpreted Jesus' death in part through the lens of these atonement sacrifices. Thus, the connection between this verse and Jesus is at best an indirect one, even ambiguous. However, what is clear is that this action by God to clothe his human creation and thus alleviate their shame is a profound act of compassion—God has not given up on his death-cursed image-bearers.

And so, while these texts may not point to Christ quite as clearly or directly as many Christians may like, these texts—and the broader story of which they are a part—do point to two key realities that create the necessary conditions for the Christian notions of "redemption" or "salvation" or divine rescue: first, the human race is deeply afflicted by sin—each individual and all of us collectively—in a variety of significant ways, and even all creation has been affected by human sin; and second, the transcendent and immanent, holy and almighty, loving and faithful God has not given up on his death-cursed humanity and his sin-scarred creation.

All this means that, in spite of a tragic betrayal and a debilitating curse, the loyal devotion of a loving God continues on. The love story is still being written.

IN THE END, A NEW BEGINNING . . .

I like the dreams of the future better than the history of the past.

– THOMAS JEFFERSON (1743–1826)

What we call the beginning is often the end. And to make an end is to make a beginning. The end is where we start from.

– T. S. ELIOT (1888–1965)

Every new beginning comes from some other beginning's end.

– SENECA (CA. 4 BC–AD 65)

Every act of creation is first an act of destruction.

– PABLO PICASSO (1881–1973)

Behold, I make the last things like the first things.

– *THE EPISTLE OF BARNABAS* (CA. 120)

Reading Ancient Apocalyptic Visions

…and they all lived happily ever after.

REMEMBER THE FAIRY TALE? THAT fictional little folk tale of magic and love and princesses and princes starting off "once upon a time" and ending "happily ever after"? That make-believe story intended to reinforce certain social values? We need to return back to that discussion for a moment, our earlier exploration of the *genre* of a text.

You will recall that a genre is like an unspoken agreement between the author and the reader of a text. The genre provides a framework, some conventional guidelines or constraints, for creating and understanding the text. The author of a text will indicate the genre through a variety of means: nothing explicit, but rather implicit, through characteristic words or phrases or topics or themes, or through such features as the piece's style or length or structure. Once you recognize the genre—whether intuitively or through careful determination—you are better equipped to interpret the text, to discern whatever truth or goodness or beauty the text may convey.

Thus, as we noted earlier, you will interpret a history textbook differently than a historical novel, even if they speak of the same historical setting. You will read a newspaper editorial differently than a front-page report, even if they are on the same topic. A Shakespearean sonnet will make a very different impression on you than a vehicle's mechanical manual, even if you really love that car. And you will understand and experience the truth of a cookbook in a very different way than you would the truth of a chemistry textbook, even if they describe the same chemical processes.

Every text works to some extent within established genres. This is as true of ancient texts as it is of modern ones; it is as true of sacred texts as it is of secular texts. And so, without at least some understanding of the genre of a text, we risk misunderstanding it or misrepresenting it—sometimes quite badly.

⤸

Revelation is certainly not a modern folk tale or fairy tale, but what *is* the genre of Revelation? If you were a librarian, say, 1,800 years ago in the ancient library of Celsus in Ephesus, where would you put your newly acquired scroll of Revelation? Should it be placed alongside the prophetic oracles of Delphi, or with the dramatic tragedies of Sophocles, or perhaps beside the Hebrew prophets like Isaiah?

While such a librarian might pause at the Hebrew prophets, more than likely Revelation would be placed alongside writings known today as "apocalypses," such as *1 Enoch* and *4 Ezra* and *2 Baruch*. These were Jewish and Jewish Christian writings from within roughly two centuries before and after Revelation. The word "apocalypse" means an "unveiling," a "disclosure," a "revelation"—in fact, the genre gets its name from Revelation, which describes itself as a "revelation [*apokalypsis*] of Jesus Christ" (1:1). The name is an appropriate one for the genre, for each of these ancient apocalypses purports to be the revealing of a transcendent reality beyond the normal experience of human beings, or at least of a transcendent perspective on the world as human beings normally experience it. It is as if an apocalypse tears away a veil that has been covering our eyes or keeping us from seeing something in a certain way, allowing us to get a glimpse of our world the way God sees it, to gain a clearer perspective on what is happening in the world and where everything is heading.

To communicate this radically new perspective on things, these apocalypses used several different devices. The author sees a vision or series of visions that unfold before him like scenes in a play; sometimes the author is a participant in the vision he sees, often he is simply a spectator. These visions are typically filled with rather bizarre imagery—multi-headed beasts and multi-eyed creatures and multi-layered voices—and significant numbers—threes and fours and sevens and tens and twelves,

47

or sums or multiples of such numbers. All these images and numbers are normally symbolic and not to be understood literally. This does not mean (as some have thought) that they are "not true," but rather that they convey truth indirectly rather than directly, they represent a reality obliquely rather than straight on; so a beast is not a literal beast, but rather represents a very real empire or ideology, for example. Of course, this means that there is an extra layer of interpretation required to make sense of these visions. Often the images and numbers are left uninterpreted in the text, relying on the shared knowledge of the original author and their first readers, a shared knowledge growing out of their common reading of the Hebrew prophets and their common apocalyptic language and worldview. Typically, though, there is some kind of interpretive guide—an angel or other exalted being—who tours the author around the scenes he is witnessing, occasionally providing some explanation of the symbols in these visions.

Take the apocalypse known as *4 Ezra*, for example, written at roughly the same time as Revelation yet from a non-Christian Jewish perspective. The author, calling himself "Ezra," describes a series of conversations with an angelic guide called Uriel, conversations that the author depicts as occurring in a series of visions. Scattered throughout these envisioned conversations are many images that both illustrate what is being said and prompt further conversation. So, for example, in *4 Ezra* 11–12, "Ezra" describes a dream in which he sees "coming up from the sea an eagle that had twelve feathered wings and three heads." This eagle spreads its wings over the whole earth, even "to reign over the earth and over those who dwell in it." From its wings further wings sprout, and each of the wings has a turn reigning over the earth. Eventually the wings disappear, the heads devour each other, and at that moment a lion appears announcing the destruction of the eagle because of its oppression and deceit and injustice to those over which it has ruled. The interpretation that follows in the text, combined with the historical circumstances of *4 Ezra*, make it clear that the eagle represents the Roman Empire (the eagle being the symbol of Rome's military might), the wings represent various infamous emperors, and the lion represents the Messiah, the king from the dynasty of David, Israel's greatest king, who comes to bring judgment on all human kingdoms and to establish the kingdom of God. For those familiar with Revelation's language and imagery, the similarities between these two texts are obvious: a multi-headed beast coming out of the sea, the

Messiah as a lion come to usher in God's judgment on such beasts and to establish God's kingdom. And this is just a sample of the similarities between Revelation and *4 Ezra*, let alone other ancient apocalypses.

All of these ancient apocalypses—and Revelation is no exception—were written in the midst of severe hardship and even persecution, and they were written to encourage readers who were going through such difficulties. *4 Ezra*, for example, was written for Jews following the failed Jewish revolt against Rome in the late 60s AD, which culminated in the destruction of the temple in Jerusalem in AD 70. This event led to a deep anguish for the Jewish people, wrestling with questions like "Why did this happen?" and "Has God abandoned us?" while also trying to survive in a new era of Roman apathy or even antipathy toward Judaism and the Jewish people.

Likewise, Revelation, penned roughly the same time as *4 Ezra*, was written for a people in crisis. The Christians of Asia Minor (western Turkey today), to whom Revelation was specifically written (1:4), were experiencing tremendous hardship because of their faith. On the one hand, the relationship between Jews and Christians in the region had turned sour by this time, resulting in Christians being expelled from Jewish synagogues and being otherwise mistreated (no doubt the problem went the other way as well). On the other hand, and more significantly, the Roman Empire was being increasingly oppressive toward Christians and other religious groups on the fringes of Roman society. In particular, the imperial cult—religious worship of the emperors, with its own temples and priests—was more and more powerful through this period and in this region. For example, it required in some instances that artisans worship at the imperial cult in order to be able to practice their trade, or in other instances that all persons affirm an oath of loyalty to the emperor, even seeing him as the world's preeminent "lord" and "god." As you can imagine, all this was problematic for these early Christians, leading to compromise by some of them, and to oppression and persecution, and even in some cases death, for those who remained faithful.

There are thus some significant—and very illuminating—similarities between Revelation and other ancient apocalypses. But there are also some profound differences. For example, Revelation is not pseudepigraphic or "falsely attributed." Most if not all of the other ancient apocalypses claimed to be visions of a famous Jewish figure—"Ezra" in *4 Ezra*, for example—yet they were not actually written by that person. Revelation, on the other hand, claims to be written by "John," who was a prophet in a prophetic community in Asia Minor (1:4; 22:9), and there is no reason to doubt that this was in fact the author's real name and background.

One other difference is worth noting. Many other ancient apocalypses described events already past as if they were yet future, or described recent or present events in the guise of describing events long past. So, for example, *4 Ezra* purports to be describing the situation following the destruction of Jerusalem and its temple in 586 BC, yet it is actually the events of AD 70 and their aftermath that are in view. Revelation, however, describes itself as dealing with "both what is now and what will take place later" (1:19), and that is in fact what it does, focusing on the present situation (the late first century AD) in light of the coming future. It is interesting to note in this that while Revelation describes itself as an "apocalypse" (1:1), it also presents itself as a "prophecy" (1:3) and as a letter (1:4). Prophecy—at least in the Hebrew prophetic tradition that John seems to model himself after—was not simply about predicting future events. Rather, anyone who has carefully read the Old Testament prophets knows that the Hebrew prophets critically engaged the situation of their present time—exposing injustice, hypocrisy, greed, idolatry, and so on—while pointing forward to a future "day" of the Lord's judgment and deliverance. And all letters, whether ancient or modern, are related to the present situation of the author and reader—they arise from and deal with the particular setting in which they are written. Thus, Revelation as apocalypse and prophecy and letter deals both with its ancient first-century setting and with the future kingdom of God, both the present age and the coming age.

⤴

The terms "apocalypse" or "apocalyptic" today have connotations of the world ending in cataclysmic destruction—an idea perpetuated by a string of *New York Times* bestsellers and Hollywood blockbusters. And certainly the language and imagery of Revelation have fed into this idea. But this takes Revelation's language and imagery too far, taking it too literally, not understanding the way an ancient apocalypse works. Revelation is much more concerned with the present world than many people think, and Revelation's language and imagery symbolically describe the present age even as they point to the future destiny of humanity and all creation. As an apocalypse, Revelation is not describing the world ending in cataclysmic destruction; rather, it is much more about human beings and human kingdoms destroying each other and the world through our actions now, and about what God has done, is doing, and will do to bring about the end of this destruction and the beginning of something new.

In a way, then, Revelation is very similar to Genesis in the kinds of questions it is intended to answer. Though it does speak of the future, Revelation is not so much concerned with the precise *when* and *how* questions of the future as much as the *who* and *what* and *why* sorts of questions of human—and especially Christian—existence in this present age: Why do we suffer in this world, especially as God's people? Is God faithful to his people and his creation? What is our role as God's people in this oppressive world? What is wrong with the world? How will things be made right?

Thus, in a real sense, reading Revelation is a lot like attending a good play—which brings us back to the importance of stories in shaping our collective identity and purpose and values. We have narrators (John and his angelic interpreter) guiding us through the story. We have a series of scenes (apocalyptic visions) unfolding before us, which are visually and verbally stimulating, even provocative, critiquing the world in which we live even as they present for us the world as it could be, as it *will* be. And, just like a good play, if we fully engage the strange world of this dramatic story we call Revelation, we will come out of the theater changed, seeing the real world—and our place in it—in a radically new way.

And so let us enter the strange and provocative drama of Revelation, considering a few of these visionary scenes of Revelation to allow them to shape our theology and our practice as the people of God holding to the testimony of Jesus and destined for deliverance and renewal in a death-defeated and curse-cleansed world.

A Vision of Jesus' Coming (Revelation 12)

A great and wondrous sign appeared in heaven: a woman clothed with the sun, with the moon under her feet and a crown of twelve stars on her head. She was pregnant and cried out in pain as she was about to give birth. Then another sign appeared in heaven: an enormous red dragon with seven heads and ten horns and seven crowns on its heads. Its tail swept a third of the stars out of the sky and flung them to the earth. The dragon stood in front of the woman who was about to give birth, so that it might devour her child the moment he was born. She gave birth to a son, a male child, who will rule all the nations with an iron scepter. And her child was snatched up to God and to his throne. The woman fled into the wilderness to a place prepared for her by God, where she might be taken care of for 1,260 days.

And there was war in heaven. Michael and his angels fought against the dragon, and the dragon and his angels fought back. But he was not strong enough, and they lost their place in heaven. The great dragon was hurled down—that ancient serpent called the devil, or Satan, who leads the whole world astray. He was hurled to the earth, and his angels with him.

Then I heard a loud voice in heaven say: "Now have come the salvation and the power and the kingdom of our God, and the authority of his Messiah. For the accuser of our brothers and sisters, who accuses them before our God day and night, has been hurled down. They triumphed over him by the blood of the Lamb and by the word of their testimony; they did not love their lives so much as to shrink from death. Therefore rejoice, you heavens and you who dwell in them! But woe to the earth and the sea, because the devil has gone down to you! He is filled with fury, because he knows that his time is short."

When the dragon saw that he had been hurled to the earth, he pursued the woman who had given birth to the male child. The woman was given

the two wings of a great eagle, so that she might fly to the place prepared
for her in the wilderness, where she would be taken care of for a time, times
and half a time, out of the serpent's reach. Then from his mouth the serpent
spewed water like a river, to overtake the woman and sweep her away with
the torrent. But the earth helped the woman by opening its mouth and swal-
lowing the river that the dragon had spewed out of his mouth. Then the
dragon was enraged at the woman and went off to make war against the
rest of her offspring—those who keep God's commands and hold fast their
testimony about Jesus.

ONE OF THE MANY UNUSUAL features of Revelation is that it never directly
quotes an Old Testament passage beyond a few words, yet Revelation is
overflowing with Old Testament language and imagery and ideas. This
includes much of the language and imagery and ideas we have explored
in looking at Genesis 1–3.

Thus, when the central section of Revelation opens with a vision of
God (Revelation 4–5), we should not be surprised when we hear echoes
of the creation stories of Genesis. In the first part of the vision, in Revelation 4, God is seen as the transcendent and holy Creator who sits in the
center of all creation as a King on his throne in the midst of his palace-
temple. "Holy, holy, holy is the Lord God Almighty, who was, and is, and
is to come" (4:8), chant the four living creatures as representatives of all
creation (think of the "four winds" or the "four corners of the earth," and
note the range of creatures represented). And the twenty-four elders,
God's heavenly council representing all God's people (think of the twelve
tribes of Israel plus the twelve apostles of Christ), respond by saying, "You
are worthy, our Lord and God, to receive glory and honor and power, for
you created all things, and by your will they were created and have their
being" (4:11).

In Revelation 5 God continues to be portrayed in these terms of
transcendence and holiness, but also shows himself as the immanent and
loving and faithful Creator who comes near to creation, even to redeem
humanity no matter what the cost. In response to this revelation of the
holy God showing his faithful love in the Lion-Lamb, Jesus, the four living creatures (all creation) and the twenty-four elders (all God's people)
raise their voices in a new song: "You are worthy to take the scroll and to

open its seals, because you were slain, and with your blood you purchased for God members of every tribe and language and people and nation. You have made them to be a kingdom and priests to serve our God, and they will reign on the earth" (5:9–10). All this should bring to mind the Genesis stories we have just considered, with their thoughts of creation as a palace-temple fit for the Creator God, with humanity created to be God's priest-kings in the world "in God's image," and humanity and all creation needing to be redeemed from sin's curse, rescued from the grip of an all-pervasive death. It is as if Revelation 4–5 is a dramatic adaptation of the creation stories of Genesis.

Then, when the scroll is unfolded and its seven seals—then seven trumpets, and eventually seven bowls—are revealed (Revelation 6–11, 15–16), we see allusions to the curse story of Genesis. The litany of deep death described as humanity's and creation's curse for human sin in Genesis 3—shame, guilt, futility, hostility, exclusion, oppression, pain, suffering, physical death—is abundantly evident in the frightening descriptions of self-inflicted and God-pronounced judgment throughout these three "seven" vision sequences. War, poverty, economic oppression, famine, plague, and death are portrayed as terrifying horsemen riding throughout the earth (6:3–8). The degradation and destruction of creation as a consequence of human sin, leading to further human misery, is depicted in the most basic elements of God's original creation—day, night, sky, land, seas—being devastated through horrible catastrophes (8:7–12; 16:3–9). These and other descriptions from the three "seven" visions of Revelation suggest the fruition of sin's curse, and so Revelation 6–11 and 15–16 read like an apocalyptic retelling of the curse story of Genesis 3.

The Old Testament is not the only source for Revelation's language and imagery and ideas, however. This is perhaps most clearly seen in the vision of "cosmic conflict" found in Revelation 12 (really continuing through Revelation 14), the vision narrated at the beginning of this chapter. This vision has remarkable similarities not just to Old Testament ideas but also to many different mythic stories from the ancient world, including some of the ancient cosmogonies we looked at earlier. The sea as primordial chaos, the land as the realm of humankind, sea monsters and serpents and dragons and beasts as the great forces of chaotic evil in the world, with great heroes come to subdue these forces, even to destroy them—these are key elements of many of the worldview-shaping myths of the ancient world, and these universal mythic elements are absorbed into this apocalyptic vision.

So what is this vision all about? There is certainly debate surrounding the interpretation of each of this vision's major symbols, but the basic contours are fairly clear. The "woman clothed with the sun, with the moon under her feet and a crown of twelve stars on her head" (12:1), who gives birth to the "male child," is most likely, in some sense, Israel. The number twelve here reflects the twelve tribes of Israel descending from the twelve sons of Jacob, and the image of the sun, moon, and twelve stars recalls Joseph's dream of himself and his brothers as these patriarchs of Israel (Genesis 37:9). The "enormous red dragon with seven heads and ten horns and seven crowns on its heads" (12:3), who tries to devour the "male child" after his birth, is openly identified as "that ancient serpent called the devil, or Satan, who leads the whole world astray" (12:9)—a clear reference to the serpent, the embodiment of evil in the world, in the curse story of Genesis 3. And the "male child" himself is clearly Jesus: he is the one who "will rule all the nations with an iron scepter" (12:5). This is a brief quotation of Psalm 2:9, a royal song for the ancient Israelite kings descended from David, a psalm that was taken in at least some Jewish circles as referring ultimately to the future Messiah from David's dynasty, and was consistently understood by the earliest Christians as referring to Jesus as Messiah (see, for example, Acts 4:25–26; 13:33; Hebrews 1:5).

Having identified the main characters of this scene, we can now make sense of its basic plot. The woman is about to give birth to a boy; the Messiah is about to appear from the ancient line of Israel (12:1–2). So we are transported back to the time just before Jesus' birth, as if we are watching the anticipation of the Messiah in the opening stories of Matthew's and Luke's Gospels through an apocalyptic lens (see Matthew 1–2; Luke 1–2). The multi-headed, -horned, and -crowned dragon hears of this impending birth and waits in front of the woman to devour the child; the ancient embodiment of evil, Satan, powerful and strong and ruling in the world (thus the heads, horns, and crowns), waits for the Messiah to be born in order to destroy him and the kingdom he brings (12:3–4). But Satan is thwarted as the child is snatched up to God and his heavenly throne (12:5)—rather startling for those of us familiar with the story of Jesus in the Gospels, as this skips over Jesus' life, death, and resurrection, right to his exaltation in God's presence. This whirlwind story of Jesus the Messiah is then recast in the form of a cosmic battle, with the result that Satan is "hurled [from heaven] to the earth, and all his angels with him" (12:7–9; see Luke 10:18–19).

A woman, her offspring, and a serpent. If that sounds familiar, it should—it is a clear allusion to the enigmatic promise of Genesis 3:15, which we explored in an earlier chapter: "I will put enmity between you [the serpent] and the woman, between your offspring and hers; he will crush your head, and you will strike his heel." In our discussion on Genesis 3 we suggested that while this promise would obviously not have been read by ancient Israelites as referring to "salvation through Jesus," there is some legitimacy in seeing it more indirectly as alluding to "deliverance from evil through Israel, even Israel's Messiah." And here we see John in his apocalyptic vision reading Genesis 3:15 in exactly this way: Israel produces a Messiah, the woman's offspring, who will destroy the ancient serpent, Satan, the epitome of evil in the world.

The outcome of this initial coming of Jesus the Messiah is announced by a loud voice from heaven:

> Now have come the salvation and the power and the kingdom of our God, and the authority of his Messiah. For the accuser of our brothers and sisters, who accuses them before our God day and night, has been hurled down. They triumphed over him by the blood of the Lamb and by the word of their testimony; they did not love their lives so much as to shrink from death. Therefore rejoice, you heavens and you who dwell in them! But woe to the earth and the sea, because the devil has gone down to you! He is filled with fury, because he knows that his time is short. (12:10–12)

Notice the *already* dimension of this: Jesus the Messiah has already brought about God's "salvation" and "power" for humanity; that is, the "kingdom of our God," God's saving, sovereign reign on earth, is already here (see 11:15). But notice also the *not yet* dimension of this: that this salvation and power and kingdom of God have already come through the Messiah does not mean evil has been fully eradicated; in fact, it means "the devil" is "filled with fury, because he knows that his time his short"— evil only increases alongside the growth of God's kingdom in the world.

This means terrible things for Israel, from whom the Messiah has come. The woman is pursued by the dragon, and experiences two miraculous escapes from the dragon's clutches: she is given the wings of an eagle to fly from the dragon to the wilderness, and then she is protected by the earth when the dragon attempts to drown her (12:6, 13–16). It is not clear exactly what this refers to—perhaps in part it was intended to recall the flight of many Jews from Jerusalem before its destruction by Rome in AD 70—but, unintentionally or otherwise, it aptly depicts the remarkable resilience of the Jewish people historically in the face of impending destruction.

This increase of evil in the world also means terrible things for the followers of Jesus: "the dragon was enraged at the woman and went off to make war against the rest of her offspring—those who keep God's commands and hold fast their testimony about Jesus" (12:17). This "war" is spelled out in the next chapter. Two grotesque beasts—a distorted Leviathan from the sea and a deformed Behemoth from the land, ancient Israel's mythic creatures of primordial chaos (for example, Job 40–41 and Isaiah 27:1; and see Daniel 7)—join the satanic dragon in an unholy trinity of increased evil in the world (Revelation 13). The first Christians to whom Revelation was written would undoubtedly have seen the Roman Empire and the imperial cult respectively behind these two beasts, oppressing and persecuting and killing all who refuse to submit to them. But the timeless, mythic character of these beasts suggests that Rome was only the immediate manifestation of many such political, economic, and religious systems in opposition against God's kingdom.

Nevertheless, the victory of the followers of Jesus over this unholy trinity is assured, and the key to this victory is given already in Revelation 12: "They triumphed over them by the blood of the Lamb and by the word of their testimony; they did not love their lives so much as to shrink from death" (12:11). The "blood of the Lamb" is the death of Jesus on the cross, which accomplishes redemption from sin's slavery like a new exodus to a new promised land; the "word of their testimony" is the confession of Jesus' followers to this "salvation" and "power" and "kingdom of God" brought about by Jesus; and the truth and power of this confession is demonstrated through the fact that these followers of Jesus "did not love their lives so much as to shrink from death."

Thus, in apocalyptic vision, we see in Revelation 12 the story of Jesus and his followers. It is the story of Jesus' coming into the world as Messiah to bring in God's kingdom, making right what has gone wrong with humanity and all creation, and the story of Jesus' followers victoriously continuing this mission through their suffering witness to Jesus in word and deed.

In light of all this, we are able to sketch out some answers to those questions Revelation as an apocalypse was intended to answer for its first readers. *Why do we suffer in this world, especially as God's people? What is wrong with the world?* In spite of appearances to the contrary, in spite of Rome's rhetoric of "peace and safety," its famed *pax Romana*, the world is the scene of a cosmic conflict between forces of good and forces of evil. The forces of evil have been dealt a crushing blow through Jesus' death on the cross, but in this time between the times, this era between Jesus' first coming and his second, evil is only increasing in the world in its scope and strength. Though sin has lost its enslaving power for those who follow Jesus, sin's curse of deep death still pervades humanity and all creation, evil is still embodied in the world—and those early Christians, along with many Christians throughout this age, have experienced the brunt of this sin and death, this embodiment of evil arrayed against God and his purposes.

Is God faithful to his people and his creation? How will things be made right? Indeed, God is still faithful. God shows his faithfulness in revealing these things to his people; God does not leave them to make sense of their suffering on their own, but opens up a divine perspective on their circumstances. Even more importantly, God has shown his faithfulness by acting definitively through Jesus: Jesus is the Lamb who has been slain to redeem God's people from sin's slavery, and Jesus is the Lion who brings in God's kingdom in the midst of the world's empires, who is exalted to God's presence with God's authority, and who will one day rule all the nations with true justice and peace. This is how things will be made right: through the crucified and resurrected Messiah, the slain Lamb and reigning Lion.

So what is our role as God's people in this oppressive world? To bear witness to this salvation and power and kingdom of God brought about by Jesus, and to demonstrate the truth and power of this confession by following in Jesus' footsteps: not loving our lives so as to shrink from death, but giving ourselves for the good of others, even those who may oppose and oppress us. This is a terrible irony that would have given pause to those early Christians, and should give pause to Christians today: evil is only dealt with by bearing the brunt of evil; life only comes through death; the serpent's head is only crushed through the wounds and weakness of the Messiah and those who follow him.

This vision of cosmic conflict, especially including its continuation into Revelation 13, would therefore have had tremendous significance for the early Christians suffering under Rome's oppressive rule at the end of the first century. But what significance should this vision have for Christian experience today? Our discussion so far may already prompt some thoughts, but let me sketch out three broad ways in which this story can impact us as followers of Jesus in the twenty-first century.

First, *this vision should shape our understanding of what Christ has done in his life, death, resurrection, and exaltation.* As we have already seen and will see again, Revelation is in many ways set up as the conclusion to the story introduced in Genesis 1–3. In particular, this vision in Revelation 12 highlights the way the story of humanity and all creation is centered on the story of Jesus. Certainly the scene's plot skips over much of that story as we know it, moving immediately from Jesus' birth to his exaltation in God's presence. But this is not because John did not know the story of Jesus or did not think that story important; Jesus' death is clearly highlighted later in the vision (12:11), and even a quick reading of other key passages in Revelation indicates that the story of Jesus, especially his death and resurrection, was crucial to John's perception of things (see 1:5, 18; 5:5–12; 11:3–12). The story of Jesus is central to the story of humanity and all creation.

Jesus' death is especially highlighted here, with the "blood of the Lamb" being the key to the triumph of Jesus' followers over the dragon and the upcoming beasts (12:11). This alludes to the earlier vision of Jesus as the "Lion of the tribe of Judah" who is also the "Lamb who has been slain" (5:5–6). As we have seen, this points to a bit of a paradox even as it spells out Jesus' role in God's mission to rescue the world from sin and all its effects. As the "Lion of the tribe of Judah," Jesus is the Messiah, the Christ, the one anointed as King from Judah's line and David's dynasty (see Genesis 49:8–12 and 1 Chronicles 17:10–14). He is therefore the one appointed by God to bring in God's kingdom on earth, God reclaiming his rightful place as sovereign ruler over the world and thus making right all that has gone wrong with the world. This might make one think of the way kingdoms and empires and rulers and leaders typically work in the world, however good their intentions: seizing power by manipulation or force, and then using that power through manipulation or force. But here is the paradox: the roaring Lion is also the slain Lamb. Jesus does not bring about God's kingdom or rule over God's kingdom by violence or coercive force, but rather by complete self-giving for the good of humanity and creation, even suffering and dying on behalf of the world to free humanity and creation from all sin's effects. When was the last time you saw a world leader or superpower do something like that?

The "blood of the Lamb" also highlights one particular way in which Jesus' death deals with evil and sin and death in the world. The phrase recalls an important Old Testament story: the story of Israel's Exodus from slavery in Egypt. This story, told in the book of Exodus, retold throughout the Scriptures, and reenacted every year at the festival of Passover, describes how the families of Israel were only liberated or "redeemed" from Egypt's slavery by the blood of a slaughtered lamb. Through the blood of a lamb they were spared the destructive plague that killed the firstborn of each household in Egypt, the final plague that pushed Pharaoh to free the Israelites to their destiny as God's people in the land he had promised them. And so, Jesus is the new Passover Lamb, slain to protect the followers of Jesus from the destruction of evil and sin and death in the world, slaughtered to bring about our liberation from sin's enslavement, to free us to our destiny as God's people in God's new creation. To put this another way, Jesus has taken sin's death curse on himself, experiencing the fullness of guilt and shame and futility, of exclusion and hostility and oppression and pain and death—and as a result he has freed us from the fullness of evil and reopened Eden's paradise, leading us to humankind's promised land.

Following on these thoughts, *this vision should then also help us make sense of evil and suffering in the world.* Evil is very real in the world, and suffering is not an illusion. Sometimes this is obvious—it is hard to ignore an Adolf Hitler and a Holocaust, or to discount your father's brain tumor. But there is often evil and suffering below the surface of our awareness or consciousness: Christians persecuted for their faith in a fundamentalist Muslim country, or the spousal abuse happening behind closed doors in the Christian home next door. And we are not always honest with ourselves about the evil within our own hearts and the suffering we inflict on others: the lash of anger toward our children that we quickly put out of our minds, or the ways we manipulate others through subtle deceit to get what we want. To reach back to previous chapters, all this reflects the deeply embedded patterns of sin in the human experience—a disregard for God's will for us as human beings, a distortion of God's design for us—and the resulting comprehensive death of sin's results in our lives, our relationships, our communities, and our world.

There is a sense, then, in which we ourselves are to blame for the presence of evil and suffering in the world. Not just "we ourselves" as in "the human race," but "we ourselves" in terms of each individual, you and me. As we saw earlier in reflecting on Genesis 3, each of us individually and all of us collectively live out the tragic story of Adam, a story of choosing death over life, a story of disobedient sin seen in destructive patterns of behavior, resulting in a comprehensive death which inflicts harm on ourselves and others. The solution to this kind of evil and suffering will only be found as we each turn from that tragic story and live out a different story, the story of Jesus; it will only happen as we follow Jesus in the way Revelation describes, "overcoming" evil in the world by choosing life over death, by giving ourselves in love for the good of others, even those who oppose or oppress us, even if that in turn means our own suffering—the suffering of others overcome by our own suffering in love. Then, this self-giving, suffering love of Jesus can work its way out from Jesus to his followers, and from each of us to those around us, to our communities, and to our world.

But this vision in Revelation 12 also emphasizes that there is a sense in which we are not to blame for all this evil and suffering. Sometimes we are targets of evil and victims of suffering and it is not our fault—neither directly through clear cause and effect, nor indirectly through some kind of "bad karma." "Dragons" and "serpents" and "beasts" exist in the world—the deep patterns of sin embodied in human persons, or in human systems of economic injustice and religious oppression and political subjugation—and often there is little or nothing we can do about this evil we experience. In this too, however, Jesus has provided a divine response, a response spelled out in Revelation's apocalyptic visions. God is not silent, or distant from our suffering. Rather, God has entered into the evil and suffering of humanity in the person of Jesus. He has even succumbed to this evil and suffering in his unjust crucifixion at the hands of these oppressive evil forces—he is the slaughtered Lamb (Revelation 5:6). And through that death, by succumbing to evil and death, he has in fact dealt evil and suffering and sin and death a fatal blow—a victory climaxing in Jesus' resurrection from the dead, forever untouched by evil and suffering and sin and death. John vividly portrays this in his opening vision of

Jesus: "I am the Living One," Jesus says; "I was dead, and now look, I am alive for ever and ever! And I hold the keys of death and Hades" (Revelation 1:18). All this can give us a genuine, deep-seated hope, a settled conviction of God's future good for us and the world, even in the midst of our darkest experiences of evil and suffering. God has acted in Christ to bring about his good purposes for us and for the world, and God *will* see these purposes through to their fulfillment.

One final thought flows from all this: *this vision should influence our understanding of when we are in the human story.* For the Jewish people of the first century, and for those early Christians following in their footsteps, the coming of the Messiah to bring in the kingdom of God was seen as a thoroughly eschatological event, that is, an event to happen at the climax of human history. Yet this event has already happened; the Messiah has already come. The climax of the human story has unexpectedly happened in the middle, the future age has invaded the present age, and now—since the coming of Jesus—we are balanced on a knife-edge between time and eternity.

This means that the "last days" are not just a time yet to come; they are already here. There is no point in speculating about exactly when the end will come and precisely how it will happen; Jesus' admonition that "about that day or hour no one knows" (Mark 13:32–33) holds true in part because the end has already begun—Jesus the Messiah has already come to establish God's kingdom. Yes, the end is still to come in its fullness; the weaving together of God's good purposes begun by Jesus in his first coming must still be completed at his second coming. But in a very real sense the end is already here—"the culmination of the ages," as Paul put it (1 Corinthians 10:11), or "these last days," as the author of Hebrews has it (Hebrews 1:2)—and so we already experience the "new creation" (2 Corinthians 5:17) and "the powers of the coming age" (Hebrews 6:5), the "salvation and the power and the kingdom of our God" (Revelation 12:10).

This also explains much of the tension we experience in the world. The world is a strange mixture of order and chaos, life and death, beauty and abomination, truth and falsehood, goodness and evil. As soon as we see some good effort bearing life-giving fruit in the world, it seems we immediately see another good work destroyed by self-exaggerated pride or self-serving greed—sometimes even by Christians. And we experience this same tension in our own selves, don't we? We struggle to do good, to avoid sin and evil, in a daily battle of the will. As described in an earlier chapter, these sorts of tensions go right back to the "knowledge of good and evil" we so inappropriately possess, as well as the curse of sin in the world, the widespread, deep death we experience as sinning humans. The vision of a cosmic conflict in Revelation 12 highlights for us a strange paradox: the coming of Christ helps us in this struggle, bringing redemption from the enslavement of sin, salvation from this wide-ranging death, and power to resist the world's evil (12:10–11); yet the coming of Christ has also provoked even greater evil in the world—"woe to the earth and the sea, because the devil has gone down to you!" (12:12). Thus, we should not be surprised to struggle so intensely with sin in our own lives, or to find evil so difficult to root out in the world. Jesus has come to uproot greed and pride, to overthrow injustice and oppression, to defeat sin and death—and this emboldens evil all the more.

In reflecting on all these implications of this vision of cosmic conflict, perhaps we can now see an answer to a question that was suggested near the beginning of this chapter: why does John use elements of non-biblical mythic stories to help describe his vision here? The answer we might propose is this: all the great myths of the world—all human stories that attempt to make sense of what is wrong in the world and how things can be made right—find their home in the story of Jesus. This is certainly not to say that the story of Jesus is itself a "myth" in the sense of being "un-historical"—remember the way that apocalypses work, using language and imagery symbolically, pointing indirectly through these strange pictures to real events and persons and entities in the world. Rather, this emphasizes that the very real Jesus who came into the world to make right what has gone wrong with humanity and all creation catches up all the hopes and fears of humanity into himself, fulfilling all humanity's deepest longings and most desperate needs.

A Vision of Jesus' Return (Revelation 19–20)

I saw heaven standing open and there before me was a white horse, whose rider is called Faithful and True. With justice he judges and makes war. His eyes are like blazing fire, and on his head are many crowns. He has a name written on him that no one knows but he himself. He is dressed in a robe dipped in blood, and his name is the Word of God. The armies of heaven were following him, riding on white horses and dressed in fine linen, white and clean. Coming out of his mouth is a sharp sword with which to strike down the nations. He will rule them with an iron scepter. He treads the winepress of the fury of the wrath of God Almighty. On his robe and on his thigh he has this name written: King of Kings and Lord of Lords.

And I saw an angel standing in the sun, who cried in a loud voice to all the birds flying in midair, "Come, gather together for the great supper of God, so that you may eat the flesh of kings, generals, and the mighty, of horses and their riders, and the flesh of all people, free and slave, great and small."

Then I saw the beast and the kings of the earth and their armies gathered together to make war against the rider on the horse and his army. But the beast was captured, and with him the false prophet who had performed the signs on his behalf. With these signs he had deluded those who had received the mark of the beast and worshiped his image. The two of them were thrown alive into the fiery lake of burning sulfur. The rest were killed with the sword coming out of the mouth of the rider on the horse, and all the birds gorged themselves on their flesh.

And I saw an angel coming down out of heaven, having the key to the Abyss and holding in his hand a great chain. He seized the dragon, that ancient serpent, who is the devil, or Satan, and bound him for a thousand years. He threw him into the Abyss, and locked and sealed it over him, to *keep him from deceiving the nations anymore until the thousand years were ended. After that, he must be set free for a short time.*

I saw thrones on which were seated those who had been given authority to judge. And I saw the souls of those who had been beheaded because of their testimony about Jesus and because of the word of God. They had not worshiped the beast or his image and had not received his mark on their foreheads or their hands. They came to life and reigned with Christ a thousand years. (The rest of the dead did not come to life until the thousand years were ended.) This is the first resurrection. Blessed and holy are those who have part in the first resurrection. The second death has no power over them, but they will be priests of God and of Christ and will reign with him for a thousand years.

When the thousand years are over, Satan will be released from his prison and will go out to deceive the nations in the four corners of the earth—Gog and Magog—and to gather them for battle. In number they are like the sand on the seashore. They marched across the breadth of the earth and surrounded the camp of God's people, the city he loves. But fire came down from heaven and devoured them. And the devil, who deceived them, was thrown into the lake of burning sulfur, where the beast and the false prophet had been thrown. They will be tormented day and night for ever and ever.

Then I saw a great white throne and him who was seated on it. The earth and the heavens fled from his presence, and there was no place for them. And I saw the dead, great and small, standing before the throne, and books were opened. Another book was opened, which is the book of life. The dead were judged according to what they had done as recorded in the books. The sea gave up the dead that were in it, and death and Hades gave up the dead that were in them, and everyone was judged according to what they had done. Then death and Hades were thrown into the lake of fire. The lake of fire is the second death. All whose names were not found written in the book of life were thrown into the lake of fire.

Birds gorging themselves on the flesh of slaughtered armies, a "great supper of God"? A fiery lake of burning sulfur, with torment day and night forever and ever? This lake of fire, a "second death" for all those under God's judgment whose names are not written in a "book of life"?

These are difficult images, even rather morbid, and certainly terrifying. What can all this possibly mean?

We should be familiar by now with some of the characters in these scenes from Revelation 19–20. The "beast" and the "false prophet who had performed signs on his behalf" (19:20) are the two beasts of Revelation 13, which, as we saw in the previous chapter, reflect the ancient mythic monsters Leviathan and Behemoth, coming from the sea and the land to bring chaos and evil to the earth. In Revelation's imagery they represent humans and human systems set against God and God's purposes in the world; for the first readers of Revelation, they would have undoubtedly seen in these two beasts the Roman Empire and the imperial cult. "The dragon, that ancient serpent, who is the devil, or Satan" (20:2), also stands behind the two beasts in Revelation 12–13, anchoring this unholy trinity of evil in the world. But this vision starts with the coming of the one who "rules with an iron scepter" (19:15), also already introduced for us in Revelation 12: Jesus the Messiah, the descendent of ancient Israel's King David come to establish God's sovereign and saving reign—God's kingdom—on earth.

As we saw in the last chapter, Jesus the Messiah has already come, sowing God's kingdom in the soil of this world. "The salvation and the power and the kingdom of our God" are already here, planted through the life, death, and resurrection of Jesus, and growing in the world through the followers of Jesus continuing his pattern of life-giving suffering at the hands of others as a witness to the world. However, as we also noted, it is painfully obvious that this saving, sovereign reign of God is not yet fully grown in our world. Human sin and its resulting deep death still hold sway; the world is still filled with "beasts" that carry out evil and oppose God's purposes in the world. The Messiah has come and so the kingdom of God is here; but the kingdom of God is not fully here, so the Messiah must come again.

And so the return of Jesus the Messiah at the end of the age is painted into several scenes throughout Revelation. This can be seen most vividly in the endings of the central visions series of Revelation, the four central acts of the drama found in Revelation 6–16. As we noted in the last chapter, three of these are series of sevens that describe the consequences of human sin and evil for the human race and all creation: seven seals (6:1—8:1), seven trumpets (8:2—11:19), and seven bowls (15:1—16:21). Each of these sequences ends with the sixth and/or seventh part painted in standard-issue apocalyptic imagery to portray divine judgment at the end of the age: blackened sun, reddened moon, falling stars, lightning, thunder, earthquakes, and the like (6:12–17; 11:19; 16:18–21; see also, for instance, Isaiah 2:19–21; 24:17–23; Joel 2:30–32). Each of these groups of seven ends, then, with a description of the end of the present age at Jesus' return: it is the time when God's wrath and the wrath of the Lamb are poured out on all who have participated in the opposition to God's purposes and the oppression of Jesus' followers (6:16–17, and see 6:10–11); it is the time when "the kingdom of the world" becomes "the kingdom of our Lord and of his Messiah" (11:15), when the dead are judged, all who revere God are rewarded, and "those who destroy the earth" are themselves destroyed (11:18); it is the time when everything is completed, announced by the triumphant cry, "It is done!" (16:17). The vision sequence explored in the last chapter (Revelation 12–14) contributes its own portrait to this gallery of end-of-the-age and return-of-Jesus images: Jesus, the king "like a son of man" (see Daniel 7:13–14; Revelation 1:12–18), harvests the earth of all those who have faithfully followed him (14:14–16; see Mark 13:26–27), and then an angel harvests the earth of all those who have opposed God's purposes in the world, bringing them to judgment in a "great winepress of God's wrath" (14:17–20).

In the vision of Revelation 19 we see for the final time in the book the fulfillment of this expectation of the Messiah's return, his glorious arrival in triumph over all the enemies of God. He comes as "Faithful and True," even "the Word of God"; that is, he is faithful and true to the promises of God to make right all that has gone wrong in the world. He wears "many crowns" on his head, and the name written on his robe and his thigh is "King of kings and Lord of lords"; that is, he comes as the undisputed ruler over all rulers of the earth, to take his rightful place as King and Lord over the world. He and his holy armies are dazzlingly white— pure in their motives and in the justice of their actions—though his own robe is "dipped in blood," likely reflecting the action of judgment he is about to undertake (see Isaiah 63:1–6). He comes to make war against his enemies, striking them down with the sword of his mouth, ruling over them with an iron scepter.

In sum, Jesus the Messiah, the "Lamb who has been slain," will return to earth as the "Lion of the tribe of Judah," to borrow the paradoxical images of 5:5–6. While Revelation 12 particularly emphasizes Jesus as the slain Lamb given for the redemption and liberation of his people (and therefore his followers as likewise suffering in his footsteps), Revelation 19 and these other visions of the Messiah's return emphasize Jesus as the triumphant Lion defeating the oppressive, obstinate enemies of God (and therefore his followers as likewise joining in that triumph).

$$\backsim$$

This vision of Jesus' future arrival is both terrifying and wonderful: wonderful if one is a follower of Jesus participating in God's kingdom while suffering under God's enemies, but terrifying if one is an enemy of God opposing God's purposes in the world. So who are these enemies of God? Who can possibly deserve such a terrible end—birds gorging on their flesh after battle, never-ending torment in a lake of burning sulfur?

For starters, the beast and the false prophet. These two incarnations of evil, these ancient mythic creatures of chaos, are "thrown alive into the fiery lake of burning sulfur" (19:20), spelling the end of the human systems of oppression and injustice they represent. These vendors of chaos and purveyors of evil in the world are banished for good in a final divine judgment. For Revelation's first readers, this would have brought assurance that one day God would indeed hold the Roman Empire and imperial cult to account for the way Christians had been oppressed and even killed under their regime.

The devil, Satan, the epitome of evil in the world, lasts a little longer in the scene's storyline. In our last chapter we watched as Satan was thrown from heaven down to earth (12:9), indicating the emergence of the kingdom of God on earth through the coming of Jesus the Messiah and the corresponding increase in evil on earth in response to the kingdom's arrival. Now we see Satan thrown first "into the Abyss"—in the ancient world the deepest part of the sea, the original source of chaos—and bound there "for a thousand years . . . to keep him from deceiving the nations anymore until the thousand years were ended" (20:2-3). As the vision unfolds, Satan is released from his imprisonment, only to be captured again and "thrown into the lake of burning sulfur, where the beast and the false prophet had been thrown" (20:10). Satan's fall from heaven is thus complete; the source and archetype of evil in the world is finally eliminated. The scene concludes with this unholy trinity—Satan, the beast, and the false prophet—"tormented day and night forever and ever" (20:10).

But these are not the only ones facing this terrible fate. "Death and Hades" are also thrown into this incessantly burning lake (20:14). *Hadēs* was the realm of the dead in Greek thinking, somewhat similar to the shadowy ancient Hebrew idea of *she'ol*. Thus, death is finally defeated; deep death—that nemesis of humanity from Genesis' first stories, that comprehensive experience of hostility, futility, oppression, pain, and bodily death—is finally destroyed forever.

All this is good news for those oppressed first Christians, and indeed for all humanity. However, the final statement of this vision is far more unsettling: "All whose names were not found written in the book of life were thrown into the lake of fire" (20:15). How can this be? How can God do this to his human creatures, created "in God's image"?

We will have more to say about the general idea of divine judgment later, but for now to help make sense of this horrific imagery we need to consider at least two things. First, Revelation normally presents humanity's relationship to good and evil in rather stark, black-and-white, either/or terms: either one is a follower of Jesus who lives a life of self-giving suffering and witness in the world, or one is a follower of the beast who opposes God and oppresses the world in order to shore up his own power and wealth and status. This is the point of the earlier imagery of Revelation that you have either the name of the Lamb written on your forehead (7:3; 14:1) or the number of the beast written on your forehead (13:16–18). These are not literal tattoos (let alone microchips!), but rather symbolic marks of slavery indicating who owns them, whose bidding they do in the world (e.g., Deuteronomy 6:6–8). Thus, in the visionary world of Revelation, "those whose names were not found written in the book of life" are those who have colluded with the oppressive and unjust political and economic and religious systems of the world. If the unholy trinity of the beast, false prophet, and devil need to be stopped for sin's death curse to be overturned, so do those humans who have furthered their evil agenda in the world.

However, there are other factors in Revelation that suggest a more nuanced view of the human condition and humanity's destiny, providing some hints that humanity's relationship to good and evil is not simply black-and-white but has some more ambiguous shades of grey. For instance, there is the tension we noticed in the previous chapter on Revelation 12 between the *already* and *not yet* of God's kingdom in the world, a tension in our current experience of good and evil in this age. Or, for example, there are some intriguing surprises in Revelation's depiction of the final destiny of human beings, such as the "kings of the earth" and the "nations" who followed the dragon and the beasts being struck down and even destroyed in God's judgment (6:15–16; 19:15, 17–19; 20:8–9), yet these same "kings of the earth" and "nations" later walking by the light of God's glory in a new creation (21:23–26). These sorts of factors suggest that we should be careful not to take some of the starker, either/or scenes of final judgment in Revelation too simplistically—God's ultimate assess-ment of both individual persons and nations may well be more complex than we are often tempted to think, with some rather surprising results in the end (see also Luke 13:22–30).

A second point to consider in making sense of this statement in 20:15 is the non-literal nature of the imagery. When many think of hell they picture a literal place, an actual location hidden somewhere in the universe where there is a real "fiery lake of burning sulfur." However, the apocalyptic genre of Revelation suggests that we are working with symbol and metaphor here. There is a reality behind the language, to be sure—those humans who have colluded with the dark forces of evil in the world will be called to account one day by God, and their evil actions will be stopped once and for all—but this reality is portrayed in the apocalyptic imagery of a horrifying eternal bath in burning sulfur. The non-literal nature of this image is confirmed by the fact that, in the vision's storyline, non-human and even abstract realities, such as "death and Hades," and the Roman Empire as "beast," are also cast into this fiery lake. Again, the point is that all evil will one day be finally and eternally brought to an end; all evil embodied in the world—whether as spiritual forces or impersonal systems or flesh-and-blood human beings—will one day be decisively dealt with at Christ's return.

The flip side of this condemnation of God's enemies at the Messiah's return is the vindication of God's people. All who have given faithful wit-ness to Jesus through their words and deeds, even through immense suf-fering, are finally revealed to be on the right side of history, blessed by their God and his Messiah. This ultimate blessing is presented in various ways throughout Revelation, but in this sequence of visions it is portrayed through several telling images: Jesus' followers join him in his just judg-ment as "armies of heaven . . . riding on white horses and dressed in fine linen, white and clean" (19:14, and see 19:8); those who have suffered the ultimate oppression, martyrdom, reign with Jesus the Messiah in an *interregnum*, a temporary kingdom that transitions between the present age and the coming eternal age (20:4–6); and all faithful followers of Jesus, those whose names are on the citizenship roll of God's eternal kingdom, the "book of life" (20:12, 15), enter into God's eternal new creation.

Thus, this complex and even disturbing sequence of apocalyptic visions continues the story of Jesus and his followers presented in Revelation 12: Jesus the Messiah will return to this world, and when he does all God's enemies will be defeated, all evil will be eradicated on earth, and his faithful witnesses, his suffering followers, will be triumphantly vindicated. This allows us now to outline some answers to those questions Revelation as an apocalypse was intended to answer for its first readers.

Why do we suffer in this world, especially as God's people? What is wrong with the world? This sequence of visions continues the outlook provided in Revelation 12: the world is the scene of a cosmic conflict between forces of good and forces of evil, and although sin has lost its enslaving power for those who follow Jesus, sin's curse of deep death still pervades humanity and all creation, evil is still active in the world. However, Revelation 19–20 moves beyond this to provide fuller answers to these next questions.

Is God faithful to his people and his creation? How will things be made right? Indeed, God is faithful, and God will further reveal this faithfulness for the entire world to see when Jesus the Messiah, the Lion of Judah, returns to earth. He will fully establish God's kingdom in the midst of the world's shattered empires and he will rule all the nations with true justice and peace. This is how things will be made right: through the crucified and resurrected Messiah, the slain Lamb and reigning Lion, who will come again to bring the faithful justice of God to fruition throughout the earth.

So what is our role as God's people in this oppressive world? This question is not directly addressed in our sequence of visions, but rather these visions show the vindication of God's people and the future fruits of their role in the present age. Having borne witness to the salvation and power and kingdom of God brought about by Jesus, and having demonstrated the truth and power of this confession by following in Jesus' footsteps in suffering love, God decisively demonstrates that they have been in the right all along by raising them to an exalted status alongside Jesus in judgment of God's enemies and in reigning over the earth.

⌐⌐

Once again, we see that the visions of Revelation would have been highly relevant for addressing the hopes and fears of those early Christians suffering under Rome's oppression and wavering in the fragility of their faith in Jesus. But what significance might this sequence of visions in Revelation 19–20 have for Christian experience today? Again, let me suggest three areas of reflection.

First, *this vision should shape our understanding of the significance of Jesus' future return.* The return of Jesus is the hub around which all Christian expectations of the future turn. This is Revelation's eschatological vision, its vision of the end of this present age, with the ideas of resurrection (20:4–6, 12–13), judgment (19:17–21; 20:11–15), and kingdom fulfillment (20:4–6; 21:1—22:5) all hinging on Jesus' return (19:11–16). And this is also the consistent perspective of the New Testament writings (e.g., Matthew 24–25; 1 Corinthians 15; 1 Thessalonians 4–5; 2 Peter 3) and the earliest church (e.g., the Apostles' Creed or the Nicene Creed). The return of Jesus is at the heart of all Christian hopes for the future.

The implications of this are profound. Christian hopes for the future do not hinge upon precisely when things will happen, or exactly where we will end up. Our hope is not wrapped up in heaven or hell or the Middle East; our hope is not defined by precise notions of how and when "end times" events will take place. Christian hopes for the future are not dependent upon particular nation-states or human systems, whether the United States or Russia or Israel or democracy or capitalism or global financing or universal education. Indeed, while these things can be agents and means of good in the world, Revelation highlights the way these sorts of entities can at times work in direct opposition to the purposes of God in the world—a very sobering thought for those who have bought into any of these ideals wholeheartedly. Rather, our hope is in a *person*: Jesus the Messiah, the ultimate agent of God's good purposes in the world. And so, even as we witness to the present kingdom of God through our self-giving suffering for the world, we await his arrival on the scene to finally make right all that has gone wrong in the world because of human sin and evil.

But is this return of Jesus for real? If apocalyptic literature is so pervasively symbolic, is it not possible that these visions of Jesus' return in Revelation are merely symbols of something else—something far less dramatic, something far more believable than the arrival of a first-century Galilean Jew from the skies?

The language and imagery used throughout Revelation to describe Jesus' return is thoroughly apocalyptic and therefore decidedly symbolic, as we have repeatedly seen. However, the point of all apocalyptic symbolism is to describe something real-in-this-world. The Roman Empire was not literally a multi-headed beast that arose from the sea to conquer the earth, for example, nor was it literally a prostitute hawking her seductive wares to leering sailors, yet these images from Revelation 13 and 18 provide telling critiques of some political and economic realities of the very real late-first-century Roman Empire (and like-minded empires through history and today!). Thus, as the earliest Christians seem consistently to have believed in a very real, very personal reappearance of Jesus of Nazareth on earth at some point in the future, this is surely the expectation of Revelation's visions, clothed in apocalyptic garb.

However, the symbolic nature of these descriptions should caution us against some simplistic, overly literal notion of Jesus' future presence on earth. He will not literally be riding a white horse, or literally be dressed in a robe dipped in blood, or literally have a sword coming out of his mouth. Indeed, he may not even come down from the skies (where on this globe would he touch down, and where exactly is the heaven he is coming down from?). But, however odd it may seem, however strange to our modern sensibilities, given the centrality of the real person of Jesus in Christian hopes for the future, it must be Jesus himself who appears on earth to fulfill the plan of God for humanity and all creation.

This vision should also help us appreciate the necessity of a future divine judgment, calling us to make radical, life-affirming choices in the present. "Judgment" often has very negative connotations for us, but in its essence judgment is all about justice—inequities being addressed, injustices being reversed, wrongs being made right. But there is a necessary logic of judgment found throughout the Scriptures, a pattern that must be followed if justice is truly going to be achieved. It is a logic that makes sense in our universal human experience, from the experience of children seeking justice on the playground, to the experience of nations seeking justice on the world stage. And it is a logic that, at its heart, is quite simple: *in order to make things right whatever makes things wrong must be stopped.*

Evil must be honestly acknowledged for what it is if good is ever to emerge; evil must cease if good is ever going to flourish. And this means naming and stopping evil not just in theory but also in practice, not just in the abstract but also in the concrete realities of life. It means naming and stopping evil as it is actually embodied in the world, in human beings who perpetrate evil and in the systems that manage and sustain those evil practices. To bring an end to violence and bloodshed, those who perpetrate the violence and cause the bloodshed must be acknowledged and then stopped. To reverse the fortunes of the impoverished, those people and factors that contribute to their impoverishment and oppression must be identified and then overturned. Thus, for God's judgment to be truly just, if God is truly going to make all things right again, evil in all its manifestations must be named as evil and then dealt with decisively before renewal and restoration can happen. This is the logic of judgment, of making wrong things right, whether for individuals or for people collectively.

This is the logic of judgment, but it is also the rhythm of cross and resurrection. We saw the importance of Jesus' story in the last chapter: Jesus' life, death, and resurrection is the hinge of human history, the beginning of the end of the old era of sin and deep death, and the beginning of a new beginning, the start of a new era of real life. But for this era of renewal and restoration to happen—brought to life as through resurrection—the old era of sin and death must be decisively dealt with—condemned and put to death as through crucifixion. As we noted in the last chapter, evil is dealt with only by bearing the brunt of it; life only comes through death; the serpent's head is crushed only through the wounds and weakness of the Messiah and those who follow him. And here is where the message of Revelation and the rest of the New Testament takes on the character of "good news" or "gospel": Jesus the Lamb of God and Lion of Judah has carved out that path of cross to resurrection, of condemnation to vindication, of evil named and stopped for wrongs to be made right, so that humanity and all creation can follow him from deep death to real life.

All this points to what Revelation's images of divine judgment are, in the end, all about. A final divine judgment is not so that a capricious God can excessively punish individual human beings for disobeying an arbitrary list of rules. This kind of perspective makes as little sense of Revelation's visions of judgment as it did of Genesis' story of sin's curse. Rather, the purpose of God's final judgment is so that all that is evil can be finally and eternally brought to an end, so that what was first promised in God's original creation (recall Genesis 1–2) and begun anew in Christ's first coming (remember Revelation 12) can be fully realized, with good-ness, truth, and beauty flourishing in the world the way God originally intended. All sin—all the deviation from the divine design and disregard for the divine will, all the deeply embedded patterns of behavior that bring deep death to our human existence—and all evil embodied in the world—whether as spiritual forces or impersonal systems or flesh-and-blood human beings—will one day be named in God's presence and then done away with, in order to make eternal space for a new era of peace and justice, for authentic and full life.

Yet the biblical descriptions of divine judgment do not merely point to the future, to God's decisive dealing with sin and evil yet to come; they also call us to our own point of decision in the present. The vision of hu-manity's future we are called to embrace—injustice and oppression and violence and pride and greed and deceit and more, all one day named before God and overturned by God to make way for justice and peace and love and truth and more—this is also the vision we are called to bring about in humanity's present. Those who welcome this vision and seek to live it out—those who name and cease their own sin through repentance, those who by faith follow the slain Lamb in overcoming evil in the world "by the blood of the Lamb and by the word of their testimony" (12:11)—all these are guaranteed to participate in the bright eternity of God's new creation. But those who oppose God's program of right-making justice and life-bringing love in the world through Jesus—those who collude with the world's "beasts," those systems of evil and oppression and in-justice in the world—all these are in danger of finding themselves on the wrong side of history, experiencing an even deeper death as a result of their obstinate opposition to God.

And so, once again, each of us is faced with that ancient choice between life and death, just like the first humans in Genesis 3, and like every human being since. Will we choose to act out God's purposes for humanity as created "in God's image," and so find real life for ourselves and others? Or will we choose to disregard God's will for humanity, to distort God's design for human individuals and relationships, and so ex-perience deep death for ourselves and those around us? Or, in Revela-tion's terms, will we choose to participate in God's program of life-giving renewal through self-giving love, following in Jesus' footsteps? Or will we choose to participate in the death-dealing empires of our day, economic and political and religious empires that oppress and subjugate, bringing suffering and violence and injustice?

One final thought: *this vision should influence the way we think of the future dimension of redemption.* Revelation 19–20, and indeed the entire book, underscores the necessary conditions for the Christian notions of redemption or salvation or divine rescue we discovered in Genesis 3: first, the human race is deeply afflicted by human sin—each individual and all of us collectively—in a variety of significant ways, and even all creation has been affected by human sin; and second, the transcendent and immanent, holy and almighty, loving and faithful God has not given up on his death-cursed humanity and his sin-scarred creation. As we have seen in these visions of Revelation, Jesus has come into the world—and will come again—to make right what has gone wrong with humanity and all creation, catching up all the hopes and fears of humanity into himself, fulfilling all humanity's deepest longings and most desperate needs—especially the need for sin's death curse to be abolished.

Thus, we need a redemption, a salvation, a divine deliverance that encompasses all humanity—all nations, all tribes, all languages, all the kings of the earth—and all creation—the heavens and the earth. And so, with these desperate hopes of cosmic redemption swirling in our minds, we can move to the climactic scene of Revelation's drama.

A Vision of New Creation (Revelation 21–22)

Then I saw a new heaven and a new earth, for the first heaven and the first earth had passed away, and there was no longer any sea. I saw the Holy City, the new Jerusalem, coming down out of heaven from God, prepared as a bride beautifully dressed for her husband. And I heard a loud voice from the throne saying, "Look! God's dwelling place is now among the people, and he will dwell with them. They will be his people, and God himself will be with them and be their God. He will wipe every tear from their eyes. There will be no more death or mourning or crying or pain, for the old order of things has passed away."

He who was seated on the throne said, "I am making everything new!" Then he said, "Write this down, for these words are trustworthy and true."

He said to me: "It is done. I am the Alpha and the Omega, the Beginning and the End. To the thirsty I will give water without cost from the spring of the water of life. Those who are victorious will inherit all this, and I will be their God and they will be my children. But the cowardly, the unbelieving, the vile, the murderers, the sexually immoral, those who practice magic arts, the idolaters and all liars—they will be consigned to the fiery lake of burning sulfur. This is the second death."

One of the seven angels who had the seven bowls full of the seven last plagues came and said to me, "Come, I will show you the bride, the wife of the Lamb." And he carried me away in the Spirit to a mountain great and high, and showed me the Holy City, Jerusalem, coming down out of heaven from God. It shone with the glory of God, and its brilliance was like that of a very precious jewel, like a jasper, clear as crystal. It had a great, high wall with twelve gates, and with twelve angels at the gates. On the gates were written the names of the twelve tribes of Israel. There were three gates on the east, three on the north, three on the south and three on the west. The wall of the city had twelve foundations, and on them were the names of the twelve apostles of the Lamb.

The angel who talked with me had a measuring rod of gold to measure the city, its gates and its walls. The city was laid out like a square, as long as it was wide. He measured the city with the rod and found it to be 12,000 stadia in length, and as wide and high as it is long. He measured its wall and it was 144 cubits thick, by human measurement, which the angel was using. The wall was made of jasper, and the city of pure gold, as pure as glass. The foundations of the city walls were decorated with every kind of precious stone. The first foundation was jasper, the second sapphire, the third agate, the fourth emerald, the fifth onyx, the sixth ruby, the seventh chrysolite, the eighth beryl, the ninth topaz, the tenth turquoise, the eleventh jacinth, and the twelfth amethyst. The twelve gates were twelve pearls, each gate made of a single pearl. The great street of the city was of gold, as pure as transparent glass.

I did not see a temple in the city, because the Lord God Almighty and the Lamb are its temple. The city does not need the sun or the moon to shine on it, for the glory of God gives it light, and the Lamb is its lamp. The nations will walk by its light, and the kings of the earth will bring their splendor into it. On no day will its gates ever be shut, for there will be no night there. The glory and honor of the nations will be brought into it. Nothing impure will ever enter it, nor will anyone who does what is shameful or deceitful, but only those whose names are written in the Lamb's book of life.

Then the angel showed me the river of the water of life, as clear as crystal, flowing from the throne of God and of the Lamb down the middle of the great street of the city. On each side of the river stood the tree of life, bearing twelve crops of fruit, yielding its fruit every month. And the leaves of the tree are for the healing of the nations. No longer will there be any curse. The throne of God and of the Lamb will be in the city, and his servants will serve him. They will see his face, and his name will be on their foreheads. There will be no more night. They will not need the light of a lamp or the light of the sun, for the Lord God will give them light. And they will reign for ever and ever.

⌣

ONE CAN ALMOST HEAR THE music swelling majestically as the curtain is opened for this final scene. A new heaven and a new earth emerge from the darkness into the light of center stage, and a city—no, a bride!—appears in the new heaven, floating gracefully down toward the pristine new world below. A loud voice booms from offstage, filling the theater with its authority, with its splendor, with its exhilaration: "Look! God's dwelling place is now among the people, and he will dwell with them! They will be his people, and God himself will be with them and be their God!" It is a powerful climax to the turbulent, provocative drama of Revelation. But this climactic vision of Revelation is also set up as the conclusion of the stories told back in Genesis, for here one sees most spectacularly the way Revelation weaves together themes from Genesis 1–3.

The statement that opens the scene echoes the language of Genesis 1:1, but it is filtered through Isaiah's remarkable vision of "a new heaven and a new earth" (see Isaiah 65:17). So we are invited first to reflect on Isaiah's vision of Israel restored from exile as a new creation before we move further into Revelation's portrait. But as we look to Isaiah 65–66, the "earthy" nature of Isaiah's vision might give us a jolt. There we find a permanently enduring "new heavens and new earth" (66:22), certainly, and the removal of the "former things," which brought only "weeping and crying" (65:17, 19). But we also read about people building houses and planting vineyards and eating fruit, laboring profitably and bearing children, and even dying—peacefully, to be sure, and at a ripe old age, yet still dying (65:20–23). However we make sense of Isaiah's descriptions of this "new heaven and new earth"—whether this is merely metaphor for Israel's return from exile, or whether this vision looks beyond Israel's return to something more universal, more eternal—Isaiah clearly was not imagining some spiritual "eternal state," some disembodied existence for all eternity in a heavenly otherworld. This is real human life, embodied in a very "down-to-earth" creation.

Both Revelation 21 and Isaiah 65 point back to the opening statement of Genesis 1, that "in the beginning God created the heavens and the earth," and so we are further invited to view Revelation's vision of new creation in light of Genesis' creation stories. As we noted in our discussions of those stories, the phrase "the heavens and the earth" refers to the entire created order, the whole cosmos, and God's creation of the "heavens and earth" results in a "very good" world in which humans "in God's image" live in a vitally connected way with the rest of God's earthly creation. The earth is God's divinely ordained setting for any understanding of what it means to be "human"—we are *adam* of the *adamah*, we are "of the earth"—and so the earth is the necessary context for human beings to make sense of our human existence, to discern anything that is good and true and beautiful. Thus, in view of these echoes of Isaiah and Genesis and the place of Revelation 21–22 in the larger drama of Revelation, when we read of "a new heaven and a new earth" we are encouraged to imagine a very "earthy" new creation, a "down-to-earth" world, in which human beings live in a way that is vitally linked with the rest of creation.

These ideas further suggest that when Revelation 21:1 says "the first heaven and the first earth" have "passed away" and "a new heaven and a new earth" now stand in their place, we are to imagine some sort of restoration of the present creation and not a literal destruction and replacement of the current cosmos. This sort of metaphorical language is common in early Jewish apocalyptic descriptions of God's coming kingdom, his new world order. In 2 Peter 3, for example, we find "destruction" and "new creation" language for this future cosmic exchange (3:10–12), but the same "destruction" language is also used for the world having been "destroyed" by Noah's flood (3:6)—and no one imagines a complete destruction and replacement of the cosmos in that event, however literally the story of Noah and the flood is taken (see Genesis 6–9). Rather, this kind of "destruction" and "new creation" language emphasizes the accursed state of creation because of human sin and the radical renovation that must happen for the death curse of sin to be removed. Human sin has been so devastating, so damaging, to God's creation that drastic measures are needed; but God's creation is so valued by God, even in its degraded, distorted state, that God chooses to "restore" creation, to "liberate" it, even to "reconcile" it, to use language from other New Testament texts (see Acts 3:21; Romans 8:21; Colossians 1:20).

It is into this new creation, this restored earth, that a "new Jerusalem" descends (21:2 and 21:9–21). The idea of a perfect, heavenly Jerusalem in some way mirroring the earthly city of Jerusalem was common in Jewish thinking in the first century. For example, the Jewish apocalypse discussed earlier, *4 Ezra*, refers to a heavenly Jerusalem as a beautiful city with well-established foundations (10:25–59), and the idea is also found in other New Testament writings (Galatians 4:26; Hebrews 12:22). This vision in Revelation, however, pushes the idea in some intriguing directions.

This is not the first description of a city in Revelation. "Babylon" has also been mentioned (Revelation 17–18), alluding to that definitive place of exile and oppression for the ancient Israelites (see 2 Chronicles 36:17–20 and Psalm 137). In Revelation this "Babylon" symbolizes Rome and its Empire (Rome was known as the "city on seven hills"; see Revelation 17:9, and also 1 Peter 5:13) but also looks beyond Rome to all similarly oppressive empires through history (note that "in her was found the blood . . . of all who have been slaughtered on the earth," 18:24). The contrasts between this city "Babylon" and the "new Jerusalem" are striking, combining first-century urban imagery with some images of womanhood significant in that culture. Babylon is "the great prostitute" with whom "the kings of the earth committed adultery" (17:1–2), while the new Jerusalem is "a bride beautifully dressed for her husband," who is Jesus the Messiah (21:2, 9; see 19:7–8). "Nothing impure will ever enter" the new Jerusalem, "nor will anyone who does what is shameful or deceitful" (21:27), while Babylon is only characterized by all that is "unclean" and "shameful" (18:2–3). As a result, while Babylon is left barren of all the glories of human civilization and the light of divine radiance (18:22–23), in the new Jerusalem "the nations will walk by the light of [God's glory and the Lamb], and the kings of the earth will bring their splendor into it" (21:23–24).

All these descriptions taken together suggest that here in Revelation 21 we are not to imagine either an actual city or a literal woman. Rather, the "new Jerusalem" is symbolic of a *people*: God's new humanity, living in God's intimate presence, dwelling in God's restored creation. "Babylon"—humanity and human empires in opposition against God and God's purposes—will one day be brought to nothing, while the "new Jerusalem"—the people of God, all the offspring of Israel, all who have followed Jesus the suffering Messiah (see 12:17)—will one day flourish in God's restored earthly creation.

Seeing the "new Jerusalem" in this way helps make sense of some of the specific features of this "city." It has twelve gates, signifying the twelve tribes of Israel (21:12), and also twelve foundations, symbolizing the twelve apostles of Jesus (21:14). This is Israel and the church, Jews and Gentiles brought together as God's whole people, God's new humanity created in God's image (see also, for example, Ephesians 2:10—3:6). Its dimensions also point to this focus on the new people of God, Jew and Gentile together in Christ: 12,000 stadia in length, breadth, and height (think again of twelve tribes/apostles, multiplied by 1,000, a common apocalyptic number used in Revelation to represent something as vast but known by God), and built with walls 144 cubits thick (twelve times twelve, once again reflecting tribes and apostles). The precious stones and brilliant décor of the city—trimmed in jasper and gold, sapphire, and emerald and ruby and topaz and more—reflect the purity and beauty of God's people, God's radiant bride (20:2; cf. 19:7–8), as it recalls the Israelite high-priestly garments with precious stones signifying the twelve tribes (Exodus 28:6–21) and the stunning splendor of Solomon's temple (1 Kings 6–7). The city portrayed as a cube brings to mind the dimensions of the Holy of Holies, or the Most Holy Place, the inner sanctuary of the Israelite temple in which God dwelt, and in which God met with Israel's high priest on the Day of Atonement (Leviticus 16; 1 Kings 6:20; 8:10–13). This "new Jerusalem," this new people of God in a new creation, then, is God's new Most Holy Place; God will dwell with his people so intimately that there will be no actual temple present, for "the Lord God Almighty and the Lamb are its temple" (Revelation 21:22).

We have already noted that this "new Jerusalem" comes down to earth: our eternal future is not about us going up to heaven, but about heaven coming down to earth, so that "God's dwelling place is now among the people, and he will dwell with them" (21:3). This idea of a renewed, Eden-like relationship between God and humans is expressed in the language of personal intimacy and security—"they will see his face, and his name will be on their foreheads" (22:4). It is also reflected in the language of covenant, describing a binding agreement between God and God's new humanity: "They will be his people, and God himself will be with them and be their God" (21:3; see Exodus 6:7; Jeremiah 31:33; Ezekiel 36:28; 37:27). This covenant language takes in not only Jews but also non-Jews—seen already in the combined Israel-church building imagery noted above, but also reflected in the world's nations walking by the light of God's glory in the new Jerusalem, being healed by the leaves of the tree of life, and the kings of the earth bringing their splendor into the city— the complete diversity of human beauty, truth, and goodness on display for all to see (21:24; 22:2; see 7:9–10).

An important undercurrent runs right through this vision, a current that flows directly back to the opening stories of Genesis: in this new creation the death curse of sin pronounced on humanity and creation in Genesis 3 is overturned, the deep death brought about by human sin reversed. "There will be no more death or mourning or crying or pain, for the old order of things has passed away," God says. "I am making everything new!" (21:4–5). Or as John so succinctly summarizes: "No longer will there be any curse" (22:3). These seven words have an importance that belies their brevity; they reverberate throughout the human race, throughout all creation, back through human history to our earliest distortions of God's design for us in God's image. "No longer will there be any curse!" In this "new heaven and new earth," in this "new Jerusalem" descended from heaven to earth, God's creation is fully restored.

Thus, the creation as God's cosmic palace-temple, the perspective on creation underscored in Genesis 1, is restored as God rules from the midst of his earthly creation, with God's presence so permeating the creation that no other temple is needed (21:22; 22:3). Creation as God's garden of delight, the view of creation highlighted in Genesis 2, is restored as the tree of life lines a life-giving river running through the new Jerusalem, its leaves healing the nations from sin's death curse (22:1–3). Humanity in God's image as God's priest-kings to mediate God's rule throughout the earth, the understanding of humanity emphasized in Genesis 1, is restored as God's people rule with God over a restored earth, and as they themselves form the inner sanctuary, God's Most Holy Place, in this new creation (21:10–21; 22:3–5). And so it is that here we see the final fulfillment of the prayer Jesus taught his disciples, the Lord's Prayer; in this vision of God's new humanity within God's new creation infused by God's personal presence, we see God's kingdom come, God's will done, on earth as it is in heaven (Matthew 6:10).

There are many other questions we could ask about this vision—at least some of which are probably unanswerable, given the ambiguous nature of such apocalyptic visions. But now we are in a position to see how this vision could help answer some of those key questions for Revelation's first readers.

First, *why do we suffer in this world, especially as God's people? Is God faithful to his people and his creation?* The *why* of suffering is not so much answered in this passage, but this vision of new creation certainly offers reassurance to a suffering people that their hardship and oppression is temporary, a mere moment in human history in light of eternity. For God is indeed faithful to his people and his creation, and God will one day act through Jesus to bring about a permanent end to all suffering. God will overturn this world's oppressors, God will wipe away every tear that has been shed, and God will lift up his oppressed people to rule over the earthly creation in justice and peace.

What is wrong with the world? How will things be made right? Yes, emperors oppress and empires subjugate. But the problem with the world is deeper than mere Roman emperors, or even world-encompassing empires. The problem with the world is that it is under a deep death, a bondage to sin and evil, that begins with human individuals and extends to human empires. The problem is so drastic that only a radical renovation of the entire creation will solve it. And so God will one day complete the extreme makeover of humanity and creation begun in Jesus: creation will be restored, humanity will be redeemed, and God will dwell among us in the fullness of his life-giving presence once again.

Then what is our role as God's people in this oppressive world? With the hope of this cosmic restoration in our hearts and minds, we are to persevere in suffering witness to Jesus and suffering love for all who oppose God and God's ways. We can follow Jesus in his suffering, his witness, and his love, knowing that through him, the slain Lamb and victorious Lion, God will one day make all things new.

⌒

This vision, then, would have had tremendous significance for those earliest Christians suffering under a Roman regime oppressive in its political, economic, and religious ways. But what significance might this vision have for Christians today? Once again, let me suggest three ways in which this vision should shape our thinking and living as followers of Jesus in the twenty-first century.

First, *this vision should shape the way we view our eternal future, which in turn should shape the way we view our present experience.* This and other biblical passages suggest that "heaven" will be much more "earthy" than Christians typically think. We are not brought up to some spiritual heaven; rather, heaven comes down to earth. God restores the earth—a new palace-temple for himself, a new garden of delight for humanity—and then dwells among his human creatures on earth, just as the first stories of Genesis depict the original creation. And in this heaven-on-earth we find people of all languages and tribes, we find the kings of the earth bringing the gifts of the nations: human identities and cultures are not obliterated, but are all represented throughout eternity, enfolded into the eternal presence of God.

Perhaps this leads to more questions than it answers. In some ways it may be easier to think of an ongoing disembodied spiritual existence in some extra dimension or alternative universe, some "heaven up there." It stretches the bounds of our naturalistic comfort zone to think of God somehow restoring the present creation to an ideal state, to think of us living an eternal, embodied existence on earth. Or it may prompt other, more real-life questions, from the mundane ("Will there be hockey in 'heaven'?") to the profound ("Will my disabled daughter be physically whole?"). On all these questions Scripture is utterly silent. Revelation, along with other biblical passages, is best understood as pointing toward a restoration of the present creation, and an eternal embodied existence for us as humans within that restored creation. But as to exactly what that will look like and how that will be achieved, we are only given hints in Scripture, left with our imaginations to guide us into the divine possibilities of a humanly impossible future.

But this vision of an earthly, embodied future for humanity does have some profound implications for us in the present. In particular, it reaffirms the sorts of things we have already seen in the creation stories of Genesis. The present creation is important—not only because it has been made "very good" by God, but also because it will be renewed by God, not utterly destroyed and left behind. Our bodies are important, our embodied existence vital to our humanity—not only because they have been crafted by God's hand out of clay, but also because our bodies will be renewed by God, not utterly destroyed and left behind. There is no support in Scripture for being "so heavenly minded that we are no earthly good," as the saying goes, longing so much to be taken away someday to some disembodied, spiritual existence somewhere that we cannot see any real, lasting significance in the world in which we live now. Rather, a real appreciation of our earthy, embodied future—as the restoration of the present world, something new yet also continuous with our present experience—should prompt us to see eternal, ultimate significance in the world as it is now, and in our life within this world.

This vision should also influence the way we think about who might participate in this eternal future. This is one of the most common questions Christians have about the eternal future. Will my friend who once professed faith in Jesus but has since left the faith be in "heaven"? We lost a baby in infancy—will we see her again one day? What about all those through history and today who have died without even hearing about

Jesus—how can God consign them to some eternal punishment? These questions are often not mere idle curiosity, either; they can pierce our hearts with their unsettling urgency.

Revelation's perspectives fit well within broader New Testament concepts related to these sorts of questions. Three affirmations are fairly clear across the various New Testament writings. *First, it is only through Jesus that "salvation" in any or all of its dimensions comes about.* However the biblical authors describe "salvation"—whether as personal wholeness or interpersonal reconciliation or societal justice, or as forgiveness of sins or justification or eternal life, or any of the other New Testament notions of "salvation"—this "salvation" is at its heart a "salvation from sin and its effects," and it is only brought about through Jesus—through his incarnation, his life, his death, his resurrection, his return. *Second, those who trust in God through Jesus—those who live a life of faithful dependence upon God as revealed in Jesus—are given assurance by God that they are "saved," that they can experience this "salvation" in part now and will experience its fruition in the eternal future.* Those who do not have this kind of explicit, real-life faith are not given this assurance of present or future salvation in Scripture. *And third, those who directly oppose God's saving, life-giving purposes in Jesus will one day experience God's just condemnation of their attempts to oppose God's will.* As we explored in the previous chapter, any meaningful notion of justice demands that those who provoke violence and injustice and fear and greed in the world, spreading deep death instead of real life, will one day be stopped. God's right-making justice demands an accounting, a judgment, bringing about the end of evil in all its forms.

These three affirmations are given in various ways throughout the New Testament, and Revelation insists on these perspectives as well. But even affirming these three statements leaves room for many questions. What about the person who has never heard about Jesus yet seeks to walk in faith and love to the extent of their knowledge? Those with an explicit, genuine faith in God through Jesus have assurance of salvation, but can we think of people having an "implicit faith," living and loving in the way of Jesus without naming their lives as such, without *assurance* of salvation yet still with the *hope* of salvation? Or, how far will a loving and faithful God go to restore the wayward believer, or even the most vehement opponent of God's ways? "God desires everyone to be saved," we are assured in Scripture (1 Timothy 2:4)—to what extent will the infinite, eternal God go to fulfill that desire? God has given his Son, given *himself*, for the salvation of humanity and the restoration of creation, absorbing human sin and deep death on the cross and carving out the path to real life in the resurrection—God is fully invested in this project of redemption. What might God, who *is* love (1 John 4:8), do to ensure that this redemption touches everyone and everything that it can?

These are difficult questions touching on complex issues, and the answers to these and similar questions are not as clear in Scripture as some might like them to be. Even in Revelation, as we have discovered, things are more complex than a simple reading might suggest, with God's ultimate assessment of both individual persons and nations possibly providing some surprising results in the end (19:15, 17–19; 20:8–9; 21:23–26). Christians are unequivocally called to warn of the consequences of sin and evil in the world and to witness to the good news of Jesus through our words and our actions. But anything beyond this—judging, condemning, acquitting, saving—is God's role, not ours. May we not find ourselves to be like Jonah, who became angry with God because God relented and showed mercy to repentant evildoers even after a strong declaration of coming judgment (Jonah 3–4); may we not find ourselves to be like the envious workers who begrudged the landowner's generosity toward those called only at the very end of the day (Matthew 20:1–16). Rather, may we be like Jesus, pleading with God for the forgiveness of others even as he bore the brunt of their sin and evil (Luke 23:34).

Finally, *this vision should keep us focused on the point—the end, the purpose, the goal—of the human story.* Visions of the future provoke all kinds of questions for us—quite naturally, considering none of us has actually experienced the future, yet that unknown future is where each of us is headed! And these visions of the future in Revelation 21–22 are no exception. Indeed, they can generate even more questions than some other sorts of future visions due to the difficulty of interpreting the apocalyptic genre. We want to know details about what this future will be like, exactly how it will come about, and when things will happen. But we need to remind ourselves of the purposes of apocalypses such as Revelation: they are not so much focused on the detailed *what* and *when* and *how* of the future, as on the big-picture *what* and *who* and *why*.

And for these sorts of questions this last scene of Revelation's drama portrays a profound answer, the eternally unfolding conclusion to the story of humanity and all creation: God the Creator will indeed restore creation, completely eradicating the death-curse of sin, renewing humanity and all creation to the way God originally intended things to be, God dwelling intimately, eternally with his beloved human creation within his beloved earthly creation.

The Beginning and the End

A whole is that which has beginning, middle, and end.
  – ARISTOTLE (384–322 BC)

A story should have a beginning, a middle, and an end ... but not necessarily in that order.
  – JEAN-LUC GODARD (1930–)

OUR LIVES ARE FILLED WITH stories, and the stories of beginnings and endings with ourselves in the middle are especially vital to how we make sense of the big questions of life. Our reading of the stories of Genesis and the visions of Revelation has affirmed the value of these writings for finding our place as God's people in God's world. Together these biblical writings sketch out a story of God, humanity, and all creation, a narrative that moves from the beginning to the end with ourselves in the middle, a narrative that calls us to live in a certain way, shaping our identity and our values in light of our origins and our destiny.

The grand story sketched out in Genesis and Revelation begins and ends with God. God—the transcendent and holy and almighty one, the immanent and loving and faithful one—has created all things, and this Creator God will ultimately restore all things. For creation does need a restoration. We humans are stuck in destructive patterns of behavior—our sin—which brings a deep death to ourselves and others and the world around us, distorting God's intended purpose for us as divine image-bearers reflecting God's holiness and love, and degrading God's very good creation intended to reflect God's glory. While we can and often do act in ways that bring real life to ourselves and others, all too often we choose this deep death instead. We act out of selfishness, greed, anger, and pride, and so bring guilt and shame, futility and oppression and exclusion, hostility and suffering and death, to ourselves and those around us. And these destructive patterns of behavior do not stay at the level of individual sins; they work their way out in wider circles, becoming systemic problems in relationships, groups, and whole societies—personal sin expanding into social evil. We desperately need a transformation, a conversion, a restoration, and this is brought about through the transcendent and immanent Creator God come to us in Jesus. Through Jesus' life, death, and resurrection, God overcomes our sin and evil and summons us to a new life, a new way of being human in the world, a way of self-giving, suffering love that follows Jesus through deep death to real life, to God's kingdom come from heaven to earth, to a new creation begun in the present and fulfilled in the eternal future.

There are many other stories that can and should be told as part of this larger story. There are stories of Israel, stories of promise and slavery and exodus and covenant and temple and kingdom and exile and return. And there are stories of the church, stories of following and witnessing and suffering and spreading to the ends of the earth. And, of course, there are our own stories which are also part of this larger story, our own individual and collective stories of experiencing deep death and finding real life. For we are right in the middle of this story, living between its beginning and its end, between our origins and our destiny.

But we are not at the *center* of this story—that place in the story is reserved for Jesus.

You may recall that the vision of Revelation 12 already suggests this. The story of Jesus is portrayed there as drawing together all the great myths of humanity, catching up all humanity's hopes and fears into the person of Jesus. But this is not to say that the story of Jesus is "merely a story," without any real basis in history. To make sense of this—to understand how Jesus' story can be both *story* and *history*—it may be helpful one last time to turn to the notion of genre, in this case the genre of the foundational Christian stories of Jesus, the New Testament Gospels.

If you were that librarian in ancient Ephesus again, and you were wondering where to store your copy of the Gospel according to Mark, say, you would most likely place it alongside biographies such as those by Plutarch and Suetonius. But these ancient biographies were not exactly like modern biographies.

Modern biographies tend to describe the psychological development of the person, exploring the factors from the person's childhood through adulthood that helped to shape their thinking and character and actions, the influences that made them into the person they became known as. Typically this is told in a fairly precise chronological order, a reasonably tight, continuous narrative from childhood to adolescence to adulthood to death. Ancient biographies, however, made no attempt to chart out the person's psychological development. Such an idea would have been foreign to the ancients, who typically thought that a person's character was established early, even from birth. Neither were ancient biographies all that concerned with a precise chronology of events. Rather, anecdotes and ideas were often presented in a more topical order within a rough, large-scale chronological framework, typically skipping over the person's later adolescence until their arrival on the public scene.

Ancient biographies were similar to their modern counterparts in that they focused on a single person, seeking to show the "real person" to the reader, and they did this by relating anecdotes of the person's life and excerpts of the person's thoughts and ideas. Like modern biographers, ancient biographers used sources, preferring living sources to written ones, and eyewitnesses to second-hand testimony. However, there were no digital recorders or video cameras in first-century Galilee and Judea, so even the sources closest to the person and events were relying on memory, which is always selective and shaped by the witness's normal human need to make sense of what they have experienced.

Ancient biographies did not pretend to be exhaustive or unbiased. Rather, ancient biographers were intentionally and unashamedly selective in the stories they told, choosing anecdotes that best portrayed the way they thought the person should be remembered. In this light, too, sayings and speeches of the person, while ideally based upon reliable sources, could be expanded or abbreviated as necessary, giving the gist of what the author believed the person meant without necessarily providing the exact words. And often in these ancient biographies, the person's death—normally the last event narrated—was especially highlighted, as it was believed their death could uniquely display their character or accomplish their greatest work.

Careful readers of the biblical Gospels will see that they fit well within this genre of ancient biography, however much the genre has been adapted for their unique purposes as "gospels," declaring the "good news" (*euangelion*) of God's saving actions through Jesus. Using prior sources deemed reliable and useful (e.g., Luke 1:1–4), organizing stories and teachings of Jesus topically within his general life story (e.g., Mark 4:1–34), shaping these stories and teachings to make a theological point (e.g. John 20:30–31), skipping over Jesus' adolescence to his public career (e.g., Matthew 2:21—3:13), strongly emphasizing the significance of his death (e.g., Mark 14–15)—all to highlight "who Jesus really is"—these features of the Gospels grow out of their ancient biographical genre. The most significant differences between the Gospels and other ancient biographies—that they conclude with Jesus' resurrection rather than his death, and that they call the reader to follow this living Jesus in persevering faith and self-giving love—particularly highlight the nature of these as "gospels," as "good news" for humanity.

This quick sketch of the genre of the Gospels helps us to see how it is that the story of Jesus can be both *story* and *history*, a theologically crafted, worldview-shaping narrative grounded in the real life of a real historical person. The story of Jesus reflected in the Gospels and in the rest of the New Testament—of his birth and baptism, teachings and miracles, death and resurrection—is the central story of the Christian faith. It is the story that shapes all genuinely Christian theology and ethics, sculpting all thinking and feeling and acting that is truly Christian, forming our values, our convictions, our actions, our way of thinking and being in the world. For followers of Jesus, his story becomes the pattern for our own stories, our own tales of suffering to strength, of shame to glory, of futility to significance, of hostility to peace, of condemnation to vindication, of death to life. Or perhaps one might even say that our individual stories—and even the whole human story—are caught up into Jesus' story, rewritten in the light of this good-news story of God become human to bring humans to God. But this Son of Man and Son of God, this one through whom God's purposes for humanity and all creation are fulfilled, this person is a real person, Jesus of Nazareth, who truly was born and truly lived and truly died and truly rose again.

In fact, as we tell Jesus' story we discover that he, the center of the story of God, humanity, and creation, is also this story's beginning, and even its fitting end. As we have seen, the coming of Jesus has brought the end of the story into the center; the climax of history—real life, radical restoration, for humanity and all creation—has plunged into the middle. But this can also be said of the story's beginning: Jesus brings the opening chapters of this story into sharper focus, outlining God's creation of the cosmos as the creation of all things through Christ, tracing the image of God as the image of Christ (John 1:1–18; Colossians 1:15–20). It is wonderfully appropriate, then, that Revelation describes Jesus as "the Alpha and the Omega, the First and the Last, the Beginning and the End" (22:13).

↜

Recognizing Jesus as the center—even the beginning and the end—of this grand narrative of God, humanity, and all creation in no way takes away from our own role in this master story. Indeed, it is only through seeing Jesus' role in the story that we can even find ourselves in this tale of good news, as we are written into the narrative by following Jesus in faith and love. It is in this sense that it is appropriate to think of ourselves as right in the middle of this story. And what a difference this perspective makes.

If we are in the middle of this grand story of God and God's restoration of humanity and creation through Jesus, then God matters. God is a personal being, both transcendent—holy, almighty—and immanent—loving, faithful. This eternal God is before all things, above all things, behind all things, in all things, working through all things to bring all creation to its divine fullness. To see God in this way is to see all of life in a new way, imbued with divine significance, moving toward divine purposes. To see God in this way is to live a life of profound faith, a life in which God matters.

If we are in the middle of this grand story of God and God's restoration of humanity and creation through Jesus, then human beings matter. God created humanity in God's image, and God restores humanity in Christ's image. Our humanity—our time- and space-bound existence, our mysterious body-and-soul existence in this world—is not something to be regretted or denied, for it truly matters to God. And each human being—whether mentally challenged or intellectually gifted, rich or poor, old woman or young boy, Caucasian or Asian, Semitic or Hispanic, or any other category we might come up with—each human being truly matters to God, and thus should matter to us.

If we are in the middle of this grand story of God and God's restoration of humanity and creation through Jesus, then creation matters. God created all things very good, and God restores all things to be very good. The galaxies, the stars, the planets, the earth, life on earth, elements, atoms, quarks, and energy—all this is not some cosmic accident brought about by impersonal forces and random events. Nor is all this merely a backdrop to the human story, or a temporary shelter to be discarded for something more "spiritual" down the road. Rather, the universe and all it contains is the creation of a loving and faithful God. It matters to God, and thus should matter to us.

And if we are in the middle of this grand story of God and God's restoration of humanity and creation through Jesus, then love matters. More specifically, selfless action for the good of those in need regardless of the consequences to oneself, a genuine embrace of the "other," the different, the outsider, the enemy—the kind of love shown by God through Jesus, in other words—this love matters to God. It thus matters in our relationships with other people, from our most intimate to our most public; it matters in our connection to the rest of creation, how we live in community within the cosmos; and it matters in our relationship with God, receiving God's other-embracing love and returning this love in kind.

At the end of it all, then, we are left with the love story told from the very beginning: the unfathomably deep love of a relentlessly faithful Creator for his creation, to see it all flourish in a riotous celebration of life.

Once upon a time . . . Yes. "In the beginning," even.

. . . and they all lived happily ever after. Most definitely. "In the end, a new beginning."

But *this* love story is no fairy tale.

For Further Reading

On Story and Narrative in Life and Theology

Frei, Hans. *Theology and Narrative: Selected Essays*. Edited by George Hunsinger and William C. Placher. Oxford: Oxford University Press, 1993.

Hauerwas, Stanley, and L. Gregory Jones, editors. *Why Narrative?: Readings in Narrative Theology*. Grand Rapids: Eerdmans, 1989. Reprint, Eugene, OR: Wipf & Stock, 1997.

Lakoff, George, and Mark Johnson. *Metaphors We Live By*. Chicago: University of Chicago Press, 2003. Pp. 77–86.

Newbigin, Lesslie. *The Gospel in a Pluralistic Society*. Grand Rapids: Eerdmans, 1989. Pp. 89–115.

Tilley, Terrence W. *Story Theology*. Collegeville, MN: Liturgica, 1985.

Wright, N. T. *The New Testament and the People of God*. Christian Origins and the Question of God 1. Minneapolis: Fortress, 1992. Pp. 38–80.

On the Inspiration and Authority of Scripture

Allert, Craig D. *A High View of Scripture?: The Authority of the Bible and the Formation of the New Testament Canon*. Grand Rapids: Baker, 2007.

Bird, Michael F., and Michael W. Pahl, editors. *The Sacred Text: Excavating the Texts, Exploring the Interpretations, and Engaging the Theologies of the Christian Scriptures*. Piscataway, NJ: Gorgias, 2010.

Enns, Peter. *Inspiration and Incarnation: Evangelicals and the Problem of the Old Testament*. Grand Rapids: Baker, 2005.

McGowan, A. T. B. *The Divine Authenticity of Scripture: Retrieving an Evangelical Heritage*. Downers Grove, IL: InterVarsity, 2007.

Sparks, Kenton L. *God's Word in Human Words: An Evangelical Appropriation of Critical Biblical Scholarship*. Grand Rapids: Baker, 2008.

Vanhoozer, Kevin J. *First Theology: God, Scripture, and Hermeneutics*. Downers Grove, IL: InterVarsity, 2002.

Wright, N. T. *The Last Word: Beyond the Bible Wars to a New Understanding of the Authority of Scripture*. San Francisco: HarperSanFrancisco, 2005.

For Further Reading

On Literary Genres and Scripture

Dubrow, Heather. *Genre*. London: Methuen, 1982.

Fee, Gordon D., and Douglas Stuart. *How to Read the Bible for All It's Worth*. 2nd ed. Grand Rapids: Zondervan, 1993.

Fowler, Alastair. *Kinds of Literature: An Introduction to the Theory of Genres and Modes*. Oxford: Oxford University Press, 1982.

Klein, William W., Craig L. Blomberg, and Robert L. Hubbard Jr. *Introduction to Biblical Interpretation*. Rev. ed. Nashville: T. Nelson, 2004. Pp. 323–448.

McCartney, Dan, and Charles Clayton. *Let the Reader Understand: A Guide to Interpreting and Applying the Bible*. Wheaton, IL: Victor, 1994. Pp. 210–28.

Ryken, Leland. *Words of Delight: A Literary Introduction to the Bible*. 2nd ed. Grand Rapids: Baker, 1992.

Vanhoozer, Kevin J. *Is There a Meaning in This Text?: The Bible, the Reader, and the Morality of Literary Knowledge*. Grand Rapids: Zondervan, 1998. Pp. 335–50.

On Ancient Near Eastern Cosmogonies

Currid, John D. *Ancient Egypt and the Old Testament*. Grand Rapids: Baker, 1997. Pp. 33–73.

Hallo, William W., editor. *The Context of Scripture*. Vol. 1: *Canonical Compositions from the Biblical World*. Leiden: Brill, 2003.

Leeming, David Adams, and Margaret Adams Leeming. *A Dictionary of Creation Myths*. Oxford: Oxford University Press, 1994.

Pritchard, James B., editor. *The Ancient Near East*. 2 vols. Princeton: Princeton University Press, 1958, 1975.

Pritchard, James B., editor. *Ancient Near Eastern Texts Relating to the Old Testament*. Princeton: Princeton University Press, 1969.

Walton, John H. *Ancient Near Eastern Thought and the Old Testament*. Grand Rapids: Baker, 2006. Pp. 179–99.

On Genesis

Alter, Robert. *Genesis: Translation and Commentary*. New York: Norton, 1996.

Arnold, Bill T. *Genesis*. New Cambridge Bible Commentary. Cambridge: Cambridge University Press, 2009.

Beale, G. K. *The Temple and the Church's Mission: A Biblical Theology of the Dwelling Place of God*. New Studies in Biblical Theology. Downers Grove, IL: InterVarsity, 2004. Pp. 60–93.

Blocher, Henri. *In the Beginning: The Opening Chapters of Genesis*. Leicester: InterVarsity, 1984.

Brueggemann, Walter. *Genesis*. Interpretation. Atlanta: John Knox, 1982.

Coats, George W. *The Forms of the Old Testament Literature*. Vol. 1: *Genesis*. Grand Rapids: Eerdmans, 1983.

Gowan, Donald E. *From Eden to Babel: A Commentary on the Book of Genesis 1–11*. Grand Rapids: Eerdmans, 1988.

Middleton, J. Richard. *The Liberating Image: The Imago Dei in Genesis 1*. Grand Rapids: Brazos, 2005.

Moberly, R. W. L. *The Theology of the Book of Genesis*. Old Testament Theology. Cambridge: Cambridge University Press, 2009.

Reno, R. R. *Genesis*. Brazos Theological Commentary on the Bible. Grand Rapids: Brazos, 2010.

Sarna, Nahum M. *Understanding Genesis: The World of the Bible in the Light of History*. New York: McGraw-Hill, 1966.

Simkins, Ronald A. *Creator and Creation: Nature in the Worldview of Ancient Israel*. Peabody, MA; Hendrickson, 1994.

Towner, H. Sibley. *Genesis*. Westminster Bible Companion. Louisville: Westminster John Knox, 2001.

Waltke, Bruce K., and Cathi J. Fredricks. *Genesis: A Commentary*. Grand Rapids: Zondervan, 2001.

Walton, John H. *The Lost World of Genesis One: Ancient Cosmology and the Origins Debate*. Downers Grove, IL: InterVarsity, 2009.

Watts, Rikk E. "Making Sense of Genesis 1." Online: http://www.asa3.org/ASA/topics/Bible-Science/6-02Watts.html.

Westermann, Claus. *Genesis 1–11*. Continental Commentary. Translated by John J. Scullion. Minneapolis: Augsburg, 1984.

On Ancient Jewish and Christian Apocalypses

Charlesworth James H., editor. *The Old Testament Pseudepigrapha*. Vol. 1: *Apocalyptic Literature and Testaments*. Garden City, NY: Doubleday, 1983.

Ehrman, Bart D., editor. *Lost Scriptures: Books that Did Not Make It into the New Testament*. Oxford: Oxford University Press, 2003. Pp. 251–96.

Elliott, J. K., editor. *The Apocryphal New Testament*. Oxford: Oxford University Press, 1993. Pp. 591–687.

Schneemelcher, Wilhelm, ed. *New Testament Apocrypha*. Vol. 2. Rev. ed. Translated by R. McL. Wilson. Louisville; Westminster/John Knox, 1992, 542–752.

On Revelation

Aune, David E. *Revelation*. 3 vols. Word Biblical Commentary. Dallas: Word Books, 1997.

Bauckham, Richard. *The Theology of the Book of Revelation*. New Testament Theology. Cambridge: Cambridge University Press, 1993.

Beale, G. K. *The Book of Revelation: A Commentary on the Greek Text*. New International Greek Testament Commentary. Grand Rapids: Eerdmans, 1999.

Beale, G. K. *The Temple and the Church's Mission: A Biblical Theology of the Dwelling Place of God*. New Studies in Biblical Theology. Downers Grove, IL: InterVarsity, 2004, 365–373.

Gorman, Michael J. *Reading Revelation Responsibly: Uncivil Worship and Witness: Following the Lamb into the New Creation*. Eugene, OR: Cascade, 2010.

Gunkel, Hermann. *Creation and Chaos in the Primeval Era and the Eschaton*. Translated by K. William Whitney Jr. Grand Rapids: Eerdmans, 2006.

Keener, Craig S. *Revelation*. NIV Application Commentary. Grand Rapids: Zondervan, 2000.

Ladd, George Eldon. *A Commentary on the Revelation of John*. Grand Rapids: Eerdmans, 1972.

Mounce, Robert H. *The Book of Revelation*. Rev. ed. New International Commentary on the New Testament. Grand Rapids: Eerdmans, 1998.

Osborne, Grant R. *Revelation*. Baker Exegetical Commentary on the New Testament. Grand Rapids: Baker, 2002.

Spilsbury, Paul. *The Throne, the Lamb, and the Dragon: A Reader's Guide to the Book of Revelation*. Downers Grove, IL: InterVarsity, 2002.

Witherington, Ben, III. *Revelation*. New Cambridge Bible Commentary. Cambridge: Cambridge University Press, 2003.

Yarbro Collins, Adela. *The Combat Myth in the Book of Revelation*. Reprinted, Eugene, OR: Wipf & Stock, 2001.

On Jesus and the Gospels

Allison, Dale C., Jr. *Constructing Jesus: Memory, Imagination, and History*. Grand Rapids: Baker, 2010.

Aune, David E. *The New Testament in Its Literary Environment*. Philadelphia: Westminster, 1987, 17–157.

Burridge, Richard A. *What are the Gospels? A Comparison with Graeco-Roman Biography*. Cambridge: Cambridge University Press, 1992.

Burridge, Richard A., and Graham Gould. *Jesus Now and Then*. Grand Rapids: Eerdmans, 2004.

Dunn, James D. G. *Christianity in the Making*, Vol. 1: *Jesus Remembered*. Grand Rapids: Eerdmans, 2003.

Keener, Craig S. *The Historical Jesus of the Gospels*. Grand Rapids: Eerdmans, 2009.

Wright, N. T. *Jesus and the Victory of God*. Minneapolis: Fortress, 1996.

Wright, N. T. *The Challenge of Jesus: Rediscovering Who Jesus Was and Is*. Downers Grove, IL: InterVarsity, 1999.

Other General Reading

Alexander, T. Desmond. *From Eden to New Jerusalem: An Introduction to Biblical Theology*. Grand Rapids: Kregel, 2009.

Pahl, Michael W. *From Resurrection to New Creation: A First Journey in Christian Theology*. Eugene, OR: Cascade, 2010.

Westermann, Claus. *Beginning and End in the Bible*. Translated by Keith Crim. Philadelphia: Fortress, 1972.

Wright, N. T. *Simply Christian: Why Christianity Makes Sense*. San Francisco: HarperSanFrancisco, 2006.

Wright, N. T. *Surprised by Hope: Rethinking Heaven, the Resurrection, and the Mission of the Church*. New York: HarperOne, 2008.

Scripture Index

Subject Index

1 Enoch. See apocalyptic literature, ancient.
2 Baruch. See apocalyptic literature, ancient.
4 Ezra. See apocalyptic literature, ancient.
apocalyptic literature, ancient, 47–50. *See also* genre of Revelation.
Atra-Hasis. See etiologies, ancient.

Babylon (Babylonia), 10–12, 19, 29, 37, 80–81
Bible, inspiration and authority of. *See* Scripture, inspiration and authority of.
biographies, ancient, 91–92. *See also* genre of the Gospels.
beauty, 9, 22, 28–30, 34, 38, 46, 62, 75, 80, 82
beasts of Revelation, 47–49, 54, 57, 59, 61, 64–66, 68–70, 73, 75
Behemoth. *See* beasts of Revelation.

Christ. *See* Jesus.
Coffin Texts. See etiologies, ancient.
cosmogonies, ancient. *See* etiologies, ancient.
creation. *See also* new creation.
  and evolution, 22
  as garden, 25, 27–29, 31, 35–36, 38, 83–84
  as palace-temple, 11–12, 19–20, 22, 28, 36, 53–54, 83–84
  care for, 22–23, 28–30, 94

the goodness of, 13, 15, 18–19, 22, 28, 34, 79, 85, 89, 94
curse, 13, 26, 34–39, 41–44, 51, 54–55, 58, 60, 63, 69, 71, 74, 76, 78, 80, 82–83, 88

death, 13, 37–42, 44, 51, 54, 58, 60–63, 65–66, 69–71, 74–77, 80, 82–84, 86–90, 92
deism, 31–32
devil. *See* Satan.
dualism, 31–32

Enuma Elish. See etiologies, ancient.
environmentalism. *See* creation, care for.
etiologies, ancient, 10–12, 17, 19, 29. *See also* genre of Genesis.
evil, 25, 31, 35–39, 41, 43, 54–58, 60–63, 66, 68–75, 84, 86–87, 90
evolution. *See* creation and evolution.
exclusion, 37–40, 42, 54, 60, 90

futility, 37–40, 42, 54, 60, 90

Garden of Eden. *See* creation as garden.
gender issues. *See* humanity and gender.
genre, 8–10, 46–47, 96
  of Genesis, 10–13, 96–97
  of the Gospels, 91–92, 96, 98
  of Revelation, 47–51, 96–98
Gilgamesh. See etiologies, ancient.